DEMOCRACY
THE FINAL NAIL

JACK CASHMAN

Copyright © 2025 Jack Cashman.

All rights reserved. No part of this book may be reproduced, stored, or transmitted by any means—whether auditory, graphic, mechanical, or electronic—without written permission of both publisher and author, except in the case of brief excerpts used in critical articles and reviews. Unauthorized reproduction of any part of this work is illegal and is punishable by law.

ISBN: 979-8-89419-692-3 (sc)
ISBN: 979-8-89419-693-0 (hc)
ISBN: 979-8-89419-694-7 (e)

Because of the dynamic nature of the Internet, any web addresses or links contained in this book may have changed since publication and may no longer be valid. The views expressed in this work are solely those of the author and do not necessarily reflect the views of the publisher, and the publisher hereby disclaims any responsibility for them.

One Galleria Blvd., Suite 1900, Metairie, LA 70001
(504) 702-6708

CONTENTS

Dedication v
Acknowledgments.. vii
Prologue ix

Chapter 1   How Things Have Deteriorated 1
Chapter 2   Starting and Protecting the
            Great Experiment 20
  Establishing the Great Experiment..................24

Chapter 3   The Nation's Greatest Leaders..........32
  George Washington 32
  Abraham Lincoln 41
  Franklin Delano Roosevelt 46

Chapter 4   The Threats to Democracy 52
  Voting Rights...56
  Gerrymandering 65
  The Peaceful Transfer of Power 72

Chapter 5   The Making of an Oligarchy 95

Chapter 6   Money in Politics 118
  Lobbying Expenditures 136
  Means of Control 139

Chapter 7   Corruption 142
Chapter 8   The Dividing of America 174
Chapter 9   America's Changing Global Image ... 198
Chapter 10 Where Are We Headed From Here ... 206
  Trump Allegiance is Baffling 206
  Taken From A Letter to the Editor 209
  Citizens Rights 224
  Government Regulations 226
  Justice and Law Enforcement 229
  Control of Federal Employees 230
  Elimination of Middle Class
  Safety Net Programs 232
  Veterans Affairs 234
  Our Role in World Affairs 235

Chapter 11 What Can Be Done to
              Turn Things Around 249

About the Author 261

DEDICATION

In an earlier publication I detailed a number of events over the past forty years that Americans should find disturbing. This book is a follow up to AMERICAN'S SHOULD BE OUTRAGED. The reality that our country has transitioned from a Democracy to an Oligarchy over the past 45 years is the central issue in OUTRAGE, and that fact is again chronicled in THE FINAL NAIL. Once an Oligarchy is in place, and control is turned over to an elite group, the next logical step is to Autocracy. The election on November fifth of Donald Trump has made this book necessary because we are now poised for that transition from an Oligarchy to Autocracy.

This book is dedicated to the American workers who have been pushed out of the ever shrinking middle class by 'trickle down economics' and will now be further left behind by the billionaire takeover of their country. The decline of our Democracy so much discussed in the months leading up to the 2024 election did not begin with the MAGA movement of Donald Trump. It has been an ongoing transition for the past forty five years. The once robust and economically sound middle class has been devastated by over forty years of government policies aimed at benefitting the wealthiest 10% of the country while leaving the other 90% of Americans behind. As the wealthy class has been catered to for four decades, those with wealth have become increasingly more powerful politically. This is a situation that is only going to get worse over the next four years.

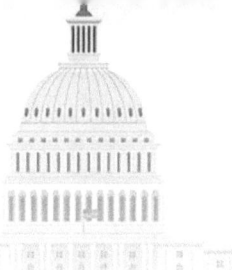

ACKNOWLEDGMENTS

In addition to a number of newspaper and magazine articles, a number of studies and reports from leading research institutions have been used to put together the data necessary to produce this book. The Brookings Institute, The Brennan Center, The Pew Institute, The Economic Policy Institute, and The Center for Budget and Policy Priorities are some of the sources referenced in the text. In addition, a number of other sources of information are referred to including the Congressional Budget Office, and The United Democracy Center and Law Foundation. The statistical data used to support the positions taken in this work can be found in these various sources.

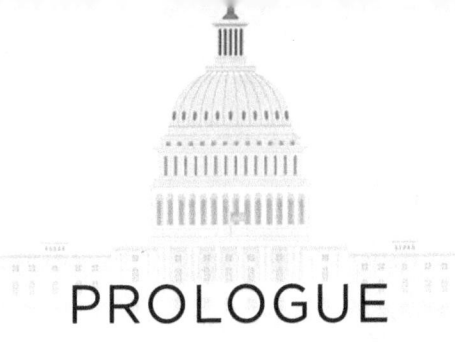

PROLOGUE

There aren't a lot of advantages to growing old. As the years go by, we lose strength and mobility, as well as friends and relatives. Perhaps worst of all, we can barely remember when we lost our own innocence. One of the few pluses of being a man in his seventies is that I can at least remember when our Nation lost its innocence and take pleasure in the knowledge that I was fortunate to live in America at a better time. In my early years I lived at a time when we still had a government of the people, by the people, and for the people. As pundits fret about the current, very real threats to our Democracy, the fact that we have already morphed into an oligarchy seems to have escaped their attention. The very gradual transformation has sadly become accepted by the American people.

Over the past four decades, the United States has become much less the Nation that our founders envisioned. Our Democracy has been on a steady decline as average, working-class Americans, have far less influence on the direction our Government takes the country. An elite class has pirated away that influence as the so-called 'middle class,' created by the New Deal policies of Franklin Roosevelt, has shrunk under the weight of the 'trickle-down' economics agenda that caters to the wealthiest 10% of the Nation. In America today money is the dominating influence affecting all three branches of our government. While Washington is asked to provide military protection for their assets in the defense budget, infrastructure that supports their investments, and a legal system that provides economic well-being, the wealthiest amongst us, who have the most to protect, are no longer required to pay a fair share of the cost. His Holiness Pope Francis commented on trickledown economics, "Their promise was that when the glass was full, it would overflow, benefitting the poor. But what happens is that when the glass is full, it magically gets bigger, nothing ever comes out for the poor."

The corporate tax that paid twenty-five percent of the federal revenue in 1960 today pays six percent according to the tax foundation, and the wealthiest amongst us pay the lowest income tax rate in decades. What's more, our political system driven by money allows these same groups to have an unhealthy influence on the very policy directions for which they pay little while receiving the greatest amount of benefit.

The changes that have been directed by Washington should inspire outrage from the 90% of our Nation that has been left behind. The tremendous transfer of wealth-creating the current wealth and income gap, the corruption in Government that has risen to unprecedented levels, the attacks on our voting rights, Republican politicians courting favor with white supremacists, and the atmosphere of intolerance, hate, and violence in our Nation should all be cause for outrage amongst us {on December

5, 2023, as antisemitism is on the rise, the Presidents of three prestigious American universities could not answer yes to the simple question, "if preaching for genocide of the Jewish people violated their Universities ethics policy"}.

We live in a country where homelessness has reached levels not seen since the great depression while billionaires build rockets to send themselves and their friends into space. This is yet another situation that should inspire outrage. The Republican Party continues to shamelessly cater to the wealthy. On December 6, 2023, the newly elected speaker of the house, Mike Johnson, announced he would only support more funding for Ukraine's battle against Russia if the administration agrees to scrap the upgrade of the IRS outdated computer system. Keeping IRS auditors away from wealthy Americans who might be cheating on their taxes is more important than aid to an embattled ally. These unhappy situations have developed over a forty-year period. Changes were so gradual, and so incremental that most Americans while realizing things are not right, struggle to understand why.

Articles appear on a regular basis predicting the demise of Democracy as governments across the globe lean towards more authoritarian ways of doing things. Even the most stable democracies, including the long-time beacon of democratic Government, the United States, have not been spared. Articles claim that large numbers of people are concluding that Democracy as a form of governing is not capable of dealing with the problems of the modern world. The issues sighted as examples include economic inequality, widespread immigration, and climate change, among others. Except for climate change, these are issues that democracies have faced before and have successfully overcome. While climate change is a new environmental challenge of a magnitude never before seen, there have certainly been serious threats to our environment that have been dealt with in the past. The issues facing the world today are not insurmountable and are not completely foreign to democracies. The idea that becoming more authoritarian as a nation is a necessity in order to secure our future is absurd.

So, what has happened to bring us to this point? How have we come to believe that our centuries-old form of governing is hamstrung in attempting to deal with the problems we face? How have 90% of the people in the country been so completely left behind, and what can be done to turn things around? The great majority of Americans sense that their Nation is broken, yet the search for a way to fix it seems elusive. Turning to a criminal demagogue thirsty for power to achieve his own ends is clearly not a viable solution, and neither is turning away from our democratic traditions. We must first identify what has brought us here, then look at how we can bring the country back to the great Nation we once enjoyed. In order to attempt an answer to these concerns and put it into print, I consulted with a number of people like long-time Maine Secretary of State Matthew Dunlap, and historian Doctor Francis Costello, attorneys, and former office holders, as well as others I consider to be keen observers of the state of our Nation. This book is a work of their collective wisdom, intended to offer the history of our Nation's transformation, and a number of suggested changes to right the ship of state. Our Democracy has already been lost in the sense that we now operate more as an oligarchy than a democracy. What's even more frightening is that we are on the verge of turning to autocracy. Once the direction of the nation has been turned over to a small wealthy class, the next logical transition is from Oligarchy to Autocracy. These are the classic definitions of the form of government we have lost, where we are, and where we are headed;

- Democracy, a system of Government involving the whole population, or all eligible members of the state, typically through elected representation, a form of government controlled by the citizens.

- Oligarchy- a system in which a small, elite group of people exercise control of a country, organization, or institution.

- Autocracy- A system of Government by one person with absolute power. Unlike a democracy, in an autocracy, the people have no say in determining the Nation's laws or in how the laws are enforced.

CHAPTER 1

HOW THINGS HAVE DETERIORATED

There have been a multitude of changes in our country over the past several decades that have impacted the way Americans feel about their Government. Much of the change has generated cynicism and distrust, yet the level of outrage has not been commensurate with the unfair treatment of 90% of the population. As I consider the events of the past few decades and the effect on the American people, I have to wonder where are the 'Armies of the Night' that Norman Mailer wrote about in the 60's. The actions that should have inspired outrage and protests are many;

- Wars initiated in distant lands for no reason.

- Unrestrained corruption in our system is affecting the highest level of Government.

- Unfair tax policies have initiated a tremendous transfer of wealth, and a decline in workers' rights has made it difficult for working Americans to get ahead.

- Attacks on voting rights aimed at specific groups of voters have made participation more difficult.

- Abuse of power at all levels of our Government

- Creation of a national debt that future Generations will never be able to eliminate. The national debt hit one trillion for the first time in 1982. Even during the two world wars, the debt never reached such levels, but that was only the beginning. President Reagan increased the debt by 186% over his eight-year term, George W. Bush increased it by $5.85 trillion or 101%, President Obama added $8.6 trillion over eight years, and Trump put $7.8

trillion more on in just four years. It has become a standard and, sadly, an accepted practice of the federal Government to spend money it does not have. The practice is objected to only by the party not in the White House and only when they are not in the White House.

In a National Election Survey conducted in 1958 asking people if they trusted their Government, 73% gave a positive response. The same question in a 2019 poll generated a positive response from only 17%. What happened in between to so drastically alter America's view of their own Government, a government founded on the principle of creating a more perfect union? In addition to the various issues already sighted we can add;

- In the 1960s, we suffered through the assassination of our young President and his younger brother, two leaders who possessed so much promise. Then, the assassination of a brilliant Civil Rights leader. Then we went through the years of the Johnson

Administration lying to us about the war in Vietnam while young Americans died every day in that trumped-up war. His lies inspired protests by America's youth, the likes of which the Nation had never before seen, the Armies of the Night' referred to earlier.

- The Nixon Administration brought government corruption to a whole new level. To be sure, there had been corruption in our past, but a vice president and then a President resigning in disgrace was an entirely new experience for our country. The fact that Nixon avoided jail time seemed to leave the affair unfinished. Other than his forced resignation, there was no punishment for his crimes, leaving many feeling that he was treated as if he were above the law, establishing a harmful precedent. The assassinations, the war, and the Nixon years proved to be the end of innocence for the American Nation.

- The Reagan Administration ushered in a whole new approach to things. While fifty years earlier, FDR had introduced an administration based on altruism and working for the common good, this was all going to change. FDR famously said that his administration would be judged by how it treated the disadvantaged. There would be none of this sentiment in the new administration that ushered in the eighties.

This 1980s President was a disciple of the Ayn Rand philosophy that selfishness and unfettered self-interest are good, but there is no value in the concept of the 'common good.' President Reagan was the first President to promote ideals expressed by the Heritage Foundation as they issued their first 'Mandate for Leadership' as he took office. As president he famously said, "The government is not the solution; the government is the problem." Reagan espoused a philosophy of love for your country but hate your country's Government. This rather negative assessment of our Government would later morph into Trump's dark assessment of an America 'drained of wealth after years of carnage.' Trump's disrespect for those who work in Government continued the anti-government sentiments started by Reagan. Of course, the Reagan Administration had its own scandal with the Iran Contra Affair, which was yet another flagrant disregard for the rule of law. The administration sold arms to Iran in exchange for Iran's assistance in freeing American hostages being held in Lebanon by Hezbollah (several of the hostages were never released} in violation of Iran's arms embargo. The money from the sale was then sent to the Contras to support their war in violation of a Congressional prohibition. Reagan was able to avoid any blame for the affair basically by claiming he had no recollection of any of it, and none of the 19 members of the administration that were indicted said otherwise.

In the following George H. W. Bush administration (the same Bush who served as Vice President during the scandal), many of the convicted participants in the scandal were given a pardon. Perhaps their silence concerning President Reagan's involvement and the pardons were just a coincidence, but there were many who thought otherwise.

- Later we had a President impeached in the house for lying under oath, a felony for the rest of us. His party in the Senate protected him from suffering Nixon's fate. Once again, a president treated as though he were above the law. Then we had a President who repeated much of the Johnson foibles by starting a war under false pretenses while lying to the American people who elected him about the reasons for the war. All this while more young Americans gave their lives senselessly.

- Finally, the Trump Administration – Two impeachments coupled with four indictments – and a total of 91 felony counts tells only part of the story of his corruption. The actions of this administration made the Nixon years seem tame. Corruption at the top seemed to escalate over the period of six-plus decades, with the Trump administration raising the bar to a ridiculous level. The damage to our country's once proud Democracy in the wake of the two Trump Presidencies are yet to be fully experienced. When it's over the damage will be assessed by historians for decades. While the Reagan years began the process of transferring wealth and influence from the middle class to a privileged upper-income class, the Trump years have begun the process of promoting authoritarian rule. As he enters a second term as President, Trump has made clear his intentions to concentrate all power into his White House while surrounding himself with staff members who take an oath of loyalty to him rather than to the Constitution.

The Republicans went after Clinton for lying under oath, and the Democrats defended him. The Democrats went after Trump for starting an insurrection, and the Republicans defended him. In his farewell address, President Washington warned the Nation about the harmful effects of competing political parties.

He warned of a time in which loyalty to the party would replace loyalty to the country. When holding on to power becomes more important than the rule of law, Washington's warning is on display.

Every day now, we are treated to stories of the scandalous amounts of money funneled to the politicians and Supreme Court Justices. The public has heard it so many times we have become numb to it all. Greedy politicians protect one another because they are all drinking from the same trough. Republican officials defended their leader even after he took highly classified documents, refused to give them back, and attempted to pull off a coup to keep himself in power at the end of his first term. His coup attempt which resulted in a riot, the beating and death of police officers, and the desecration of our National Capital, yet it has all been forgiven. Their misplaced loyalty has given the country an example of extreme party loyalty, replacing the traditional oath to support the constitution. The Republican Party's disgraced leader was elected again in 2024 for the office of President with the full support of Republican Party leaders as well as a clear majority of the party's rank and file. The fact that someone who has said and done the many things the entire country has witnessed from Trump, can be elected to the highest office in America is the most disturbing event of all.

A Brookings Institute survey of political scientists in 2018 ranked Trump 'last in overall greatness' as a President, yet he was elected to a second term by a healthy margin in 2024. He claimed to have done nothing wrong, and in spite of the crime spree that he committed right in front of their eyes, and despite all the evidence to the contrary, his MAGA followers as well as a majority of the public believed him. The loyalty to this mendacious demagogue is as frightening as it is difficult to understand.

Why? A simple question, why were Trump's actions not condemned by men and women in power? Why did people refuse to believe what they witnessed? The answer is simple. People refuse to see the wrongdoing because they no longer trust their Government, so when a demagogue tells them he is not the criminal, he's the victim, a majority of the public believes it. As for the people in power, they simply want to hold onto that power. It's all that matters to them, and if allegiance to a criminal demagogue helps achieve that objective, so be it. Today's leaders (and I use that term loosely) are only concerned with maintaining their power and the money that goes with the job. Governing is a lost art that holds little interest for today's office holders. For many holding office today, it is far more important to get the job, and to hold the job, than it is to do the job.

I was fortunate enough to be elected to public office in the 1980s. I remember well that whenever my father thought I was getting a bit impressed with myself, he would remind me, 'You are a public servant, there to serve the public – no more, no less.' How many Americans today believe that the elected officials in Washington see themselves as 'public servants? They see themselves as a ruling class, above the law, answerable to no one.

Trump has claimed as much in a court of law, arguing that he has 'total immunity' from prosecution by virtue of his election to the office of President. The claim was presented in the U.S. District Court for the District of Columbia in front of Judge Chutkan who was presiding over the trial involving the Trump inspired insurrection. Judge Chutkan wasted little time in dismissing the absurd claim. Her ruling was appealed by Trump's legal team to the Circuit court of Appeals. In a scathing 57 page unanimous opinion, the three Judge panel wrote that a former president had to face charges for illegal actions taken during their presidency. They ruled that the public interest in holding a potentially criminal president accountable outweighed any chilling effect on the office.

"We cannot accept that the office of President places its former occupants above the law for all time. Former President Trump lacked any lawful discretionary authority to defy federal criminal law and he is answerable in court for his conduct."

As Trump sought desperately to delay his trial the Appeals Court made clear in its ruling that the trial should proceed. "We conclude that the interest in criminal accountability, held by both the public and Executive Branch, outweighs the potential risks of chilling Presidential action and permitting vexatious litigation. We have balanced the former President Trump's asserted interests in executive immunity against the vital public interests that favor allowing the prosecution to proceed."

The Appeals Court ruling was so thorough and unambiguous that it was thought by many that the Supreme Court would refuse to hear the appeal by Trump's legal team. After all, Prosecutor Jack Smith had requested a ruling on the question from the Supreme Court months earlier and the Court had not taken up the issue. That refusal was seen as proof that the high court considered the question frivolous. Those assumptions were proven to be wrong as the High Court took up the question.

In a decision that removed any doubt that the Roberts Court had any interest in administering impartial justice, any doubt that the Court was now anything but a partisan political organization, the high Court took up the appeal. They not only took it up they unapologetically slow walked their decision in order to provide the disgraced ex-president with the delay of his trial that he desperately wanted.

In a decision that shocked legal scholars, historians, and political scientists around the nation the Supreme Court ruled in a 6 to 3 decision that the President {at least this one} held a degree of immunity. They ruled that a president has absolute immunity from criminal prosecution for certain official acts within the president's "conclusive and preclusive authority."

They further ruled that in instances of prosecution the burden of proof falls on the government to show that their actions "would pose no dangers of intrusion on the authority and functions of the executive branch."

Thus the court ruled that the centuries old claim that in America nobody is above the law was no longer true. In her minority opinion, Justice Sonia Sotomayor wrote; "because the Constitution does not shield a former President from answering for criminal and treasonous acts, I dissent." She further stated that the majority relied solely on "its own misguided wisdom" in giving the former President immunity, that the ruling "reshaped the institution of the presidency, making a mockery" of the constitutional principle that no man is above the law. She feared for the disastrous consequences for the "presidency and our democracy."

As if to demonstrate the consequences even before Justice Sotomayors warning, Congressman Jordan of Ohio attempted to bring criminal charges against Hunter Biden, son of the President, for not responding properly to a Congressional Subpoena. However, Jordan completely ignored a Congressional Subpoena that was served on him months before the Biden subpoena. Apparently, Jordon was using the same 'elected official immunity' that Trump claimed. All of this type of hypocrisy is irrelevant and has no effect on electability because today's politicians know that with enough money in their campaign coffers, they can buy enough television time to twist enough truths to get re-elected no matter how their actions in office may have run contrary to the public good.

We have drifted far away from the ideals on which this country was founded to the point that our very Democracy is lost. The past forty years have seen a gradual erosion of the great Democracy people my age grew up enjoying.

The ever widening wealth and income gap has been a major factor in the loss of our democratic principles. The current state of economic inequality has not happened by accident. It has been a well-planned and well-executed movement by one of our major political parties, beginning with the Reagan Administration and the original 'Mandate for Leadership' from the Heritage Foundation. It is also no accident, as will be shown later, that the

DEMOCRACY

Republican Party has successfully attacked voting rights and done it with the support of the judicial system.

Democrats do not have clean hands in the demise of our principles either. They participate enthusiastically in the obscene role money now plays in our political process, and they are willing partners in the rampant practice of gerrymandering. Still, Republicans have led the way in enacting policies that cater to the wealthy. These policies have resulted in the creation of a monstrous economic inequality that is now beyond the control of the Republicans who created the situation. The privileged wealth class created with the top 10% of the wealthiest Americans has been coupled with an increasing opportunity for them to use their wealth to influence policymaking to further their interests. The money from this wealthy class has become so important to the objective of maintaining power that politicians from both parties have become as addicted as heroin addicts. The undemocratic actions taken over the past forty-plus years have one goal, one purpose, to gain and hold power. The role of money in achieving that one goal has made it impossible to shake the addiction.

The appointment of 'conservative' judges, particularly at the Supreme Court level, has very little to do with issues like guns, or abortions. The lip service paid to these and other social issues is only meant to hide the real purpose. Conservative judges are needed to ensure a court that supports the money in politics, as well as the attacks on our voting rights that will keep the right politicians in power. The appointments are meant to keep the judicial branch out of the way so it does not interfere with the further corruption of our Democracy. Our Judicial system, led by the corrupt Robert's Supreme Court, has performed admirably in achieving their dual purpose.

Our Nation has reached a point where our Democracy may have already been lost. The level of corruption in our system has become acceptable to far too many Americans, and the level of distrust and division today are crippling our country. It may be that we are lost to the point that we cannot get it back. The pervasive greed that drives this train may be impossible to overcome. Before attempting to correct the situation, it is useful to examine the intentions of our past leaders who built our democracy. It is also useful to examine how the corruption has progressed over forty plus years.

CHAPTER 2

STARTING AND PROTECTING THE GREAT EXPERIMENT

Threats to Democracy are not a recent phenomenon. Efforts to subvert democratic principles have been ongoing in democratic countries around the world for years. The efforts often gain steam when driven by events like difficult economic times or debates over issues that are particularly controversial like slavery.

Whats troubling today is the rather intense efforts to attack the principles of the world's oldest, most successful Democratic system, the United States. During times such as these, it is useful to look back at the forming of the "Great Experiment" and to the actions of past Presidents who have faced serious threats to the system of Government founded in 1776.

There have been forty-six Presidents of the United States over the country's nearly two-hundred-and-fifty-year history, and we just elected number forty seven. While the list of Presidents is long, most would agree that the number of truly great Presidents would make up a much shorter list. The makeup of that short list would vary from one person's opinion to another. However, the three names that would appear on 90% of those short lists would be George Washington, Abraham Lincoln, and Franklin Delano Roosevelt.

To be sure, there are other names that would be on most lists, Theodore Roosevelt and Dwight Eisenhower for example, but in this book we will review just three as we examine the founding of our Democracy and two periods in our history in which Democracy faced its greatest threat. Difficult challenges are often responsible for making great leaders. These three presidents faced extremely difficult times. They all rose to the occasion to face their challenges so this 'great experiment 'could survive. Their actions first to establish our Democracy, then on two occasions to save it, are all being subverted today.

Today, the country faces perhaps the greatest threat to the ideals of our Democracy of any period since the Civil War. Efforts over the past forty years have already largely achieved success in transforming a democracy that men and women have died to protect. A case can be made, and will be made in this book, that our Democracy has already transitioned into an oligarchy. The scandalous amounts of money channeled into our political system have given an unhealthy control of our Government to the wealthiest individuals and corporations in America. Their level of control, and how it is used, will be explained in a future chapter. How have we come to be in the place we find ourselves? How have the works of these three presidents, first to establish the Constitutional Republic and then to save it from previous peril, been lost? What steps are necessary at this hour to once again face a threat to our democratic values?

The current threat is very complex and is multifaceted. A system has evolved either by accident or design that lends support to those who seek to cripple our long-standing values. Changes in the broadcast media, as well as the advent of social media, have created two avenues of support for those who seek to subvert Democracy. These changes in the media have provided for a flood of misinformation being continually broadcast to the American people. This supply of false information has played a large role in how we have arrived at this point.

Moneyed interests have also been a driving force in the way we have reached this stage. The changes that need to be considered to right the ship of state will involve challenges to the moneyed interests. If our Nation is to address the great world challenges of today there needs to be a number of changes to bring us back to a time when our leaders were more concerned with principles than power, a time when money was not the determining factor in decision-making, a time when it was a government 'of the people.'

ESTABLISHING THE GREAT EXPERIMENT

The United States of America became the first Nation to break away from the rule of Great Britain and gain independence through revolution. It would be more than one hundred and forty years before Ireland became the second. The founding fathers, in declaring the independence of the United States, established a number of ideals for the new Nation. The five-member Committee appointed by the Continental Congress to draft a statement of independence for the colonies included Thomas Jefferson, John Adams, Benjamin Franklin, Roger Sherman, and Robert Livingston. This Committee stated clearly that the intention was to create a nation "conceived in liberty, where all men were created equal endowed by their creator with certain unalienable rights of life, liberty, and pursuit of happiness." Perhaps the most important principle amongst a long list is that all the just powers of the new Government would be derived from the 'consent of the governed.' In The Federalist, James Madison described pure Democracy as the people representing themselves in a town meeting. On the larger scale, Democracy relies on elected officials. Obviously, the right to vote {under attack today} was the key to justifying the authority of elected officials as free and fair elections would choose the decision makers.

The declaration drafted by the five-member Committee was adopted in 1776. Eleven years later, the Constitutional Convention finished the work of establishing the framework of the new Government with the intention of creating a 'more perfect union'. A bill of rights established the protections of the citizens for freedom of speech, assembly, religion, and from unnecessary search and seizure. The founding fathers had established a new country built on a foundation of sacred ideals. The ideals of the Democracy they formed were embodied in the constitution, forever to be honored by the ruling government.

The founding fathers certainly were influenced by the age of reason, the enlightenment period that swept through Europe in the seventeenth and eighteenth centuries bringing reform to Britain and eventually revolution to France. However, there were other even more important influences that shaped their thinking.

The writings of Voltaire and John Locke were well-read by the framers who produced their own stamp on the critique of the authoritarian state with the writings of Thomas Jefferson and Thomas Paine. Thomas Paine served as the intellectual force of the founders, espousing the value of natural rights in a political democracy. While a self-educated intellectual, Paine's written works provided the rationale for the American Revolution. The shedding of blood and the pledging of their lives for the idea of freedom from authoritarian rule is what drove our founding fathers. This is the same type of authoritarian rule that, judging by our most recent election, a good number of Americans seem ready to embrace today.

In his pamphlet Common Sense, Thomas Paine stated in bold terms that the cause of American independence, the need to separate from Britain, was about much more than taxes. In language readily understandable to all, he argued against the principles of Monarchy and autocracy in favor of a system of democratic governance. Paine did not stop with 'Common Sense'. He went on to write 'The Rights of Man' and the 'American Crises' in which he expressed his philosophy that the Government's role is to safeguard the natural rights of its people.

In his writings, he offered a blueprint for a more decent order in society, which was a rallying cry for human liberty. He made clear his distaste for all forms of Monarchy and autocracy, describing them as systems that retard society rather than advancing it. The public reaction to his offerings changed the focus of the American Revolution.

He wanted a complete break from the idea of a privileged class, stating, "I believe in a revolution founded on the rights of man that would end the ranks of the privileged who consider the people as an inferior and degraded mass only made for their convenience and amusement." One need not wonder how Paine, or any of the other founders of our Nation, would view the privileged, wealthy class we have created in today's America. There would have been no support for the ideals of 'trickle down economics' amongst our founding fathers.

Paine made clear that he believed that Government in its best state is a necessary evil, but that the 'best state' was in the democratic form. What's more, as a non-slave owner, he argued for the inclusion of language supporting the abolition of slavery in the Declaration of Independence. In hindsight, such an inclusion may have avoided the Civil War.

In his excellent award-winning book, "First Principles," Thomas Ricks, while not dismissing the influence of the European Enlightenment, makes the case that the greater influence on the founders of the country came from what they learned from the ancient Greeks and Romans. Ricks points out that the majority of our founding fathers, including three of the first four Presidents, were highly educated men. Only Washington, out of our early presidents, lacked a formal education. He learned from observation and experience. Degrees from Harvard, Princeton, and William and Mary were common among the framers. Their formal education included exposure to Aristotle's Politics and the speeches of Cato and Cicero. They studied the Magna Carta, learning of its promises of protection of rights. Protecting the rights of the citizens from the government they were designing was of primary importance, an important principle to keep in mind today.

All these influences went into the forming of the "more perfect union." However, the great experiment also bore the stamp of originality. This would be a central government of three co-equal branches providing the 'checks and balances' against absolute power envisioned by Monroe. The thirteen states would have their own governing bodies operating with their own autonomy. Decisions at the local level would be made by a direct democratic process, as Madison envisioned. In contrast, at the higher level, decision-making would be handled by officials elected by the people. In all cases and at all levels, the power exercised by the Government would come from the "consent of the people." That consent would be reflected in a free and fair electoral process. The process and the citizen's right to vote were to be the foundation of authority.

The great experiment was then established with these guiding principles. It was a unique, and unprecedented form of governing, a bold experiment. While today it seems to be taken for granted that these privileges and rights enjoyed by American citizens will forever be ours, there are no guarantees. The founders knew full well that history held few if any, examples of this type of democratic representative Government lasting longer than a century. They envisioned future challenges, so the precedent set in the early years of the new republic would be of paramount importance in facing these future challenges. They knew it was a system that would constantly need to be renewed and re-enforced. The all-important implementation of these lofty ideals, the establishment of the all-important precedent, and the direction of this new Government was placed in the hands of our first President, George Washington.

CHAPTER 3

THE NATION'S GREATEST LEADERS

GEORGE WASHINGTON

In establishing the role of the President, Washington had no pattern or precedent to follow. He would be the first practitioner of the bold experiment. Indeed, that was the case, as he played a major role in defining the functions of the new Government. He set the precedent for everything from the forming of the first cabinet to the social functions of the head of state.

The constitution established the executive branch as having only two elected positions, the President and Vice President. All other officials were to be appointed. Washington's first cabinet consisted of just four heads of executive departments, the Secretary of State, the Secretary of War, the Secretary of the Treasury, and the Attorney General. Working with these four advisers, Washington would define the duties of his office. He would set the tone for the real-time implementation of the new democracy.

In his inaugural address, he promised to be "a good steward of the experiment," a phrase that demonstrated his understanding that the 'experiment' would always be a work in progress. It would always face challenges that leaders would have to address. The phrase also demonstrated his vision of the Presidency as a servant of the people, not a 'crowned head of state with special privileges.' He set the precedent of serving only two terms, which established the idea that service to the nation should be a temporary obligation. The weighty responsibility of administering the new democracy should be accepted for a period of time and then passed on to others. The founders saw public service as a temporary obligation to be undertaken, not as a lifetime occupation. The idea that elected office, from the Presidency on down, should be held in the hands of a select few for extended periods was different from the vision of the founders of the nation. Public service being a temporary obligation is totally foreign to the 'public servants' occupying congress today. The main focus, the main purpose of today's elected officials is to get re-elected, and hold on to the power that goes with the office. To reassert the vision of temporary service would require term limits to be established in law. The majority of today's officeholders will do anything to hold onto power. Giving it up voluntarily would be a rare, noble gesture seldom seen in today's America.

The first great threat to the stability of the new Government during Washington's Presidency was the Whiskey Rebellion. It was a direct challenge to the authority of the newly elected federal Government to raise money through taxation. A new tax on distilled spirits was enacted to help retire the cost of the Revolutionary War. Bills had to be paid, and there was no concept yet of a permanent national debt. That dishonest practice would have to wait until the 1980's to become routine. Responsible leaders would for centuries pay the governments bills, a lost art today. A tax on the discretionary expenditures for spirits seemed an appropriate avenue to deal with the debt. Farmers in Western Pennsylvania objected to the tax as placing an undue burden on them. More importantly, they also felt the tax as structured showed favoritism to the larger distillers in the east, adding a regional aspect to the dispute. The regional nature of the battle represented a challenge to the strength of the Union. There was widespread refusal in western Pennsylvania to pay the tax, as well as threats to the officials sent to make the collections. The new President and his advisors feared that this type of factionalism threatened the Union.

Being a man of action, Washington organized a militia force to put down the rebellion. He even chose to lead the militia into action while advising citizens not to 'give comfort to the insurgents,' as he classified those who challenged the authority of the new Government. It was the first major test of the Union of States and a precedent-setting event for the new democracy. The fact that the new president referred to the upstart group who refused to pay the tax as 'insurgents' demonstrates Washington's feelings as to the legitimacy of the authority of the central Government. +It was a classic example of Washington's determination to stabilize the new democratic Government. As his Secretary of the Treasury, Alexander Hamilton, put it at the time, "Shall the general will of the people prevail or the will of a faction." In a democracy, the general will of the people should prevail, and Washington was determined that it would. Furthermore, he was determined to demonstrate that regional differences would not be allowed to threaten the newly formed Union.

It would not be the last time regional differences threatened the Union. Washington's actions set a very important precedent that such regional disputes would not be allowed to prevail. As we deal today with the genuine divisions in our country, it is important to keep in mind the determination of our founders that the Union should be held together. This would become even more apparent in the actions of President Lincoln decades later.

There were other instances of unrest that challenged the authority of the newly formed federal Government, such as the signing of the Jay Treaty that inspired protests in several states. The treaty covered several remaining disputes with Britain following the Treaty of Paris, which ended the revolution. It was highly divisive politically, resulting in the establishment of the partisan division between the Federalists (led by Washington and Hamilton) and the Jeffersonian Republicans. In this, as in every case, Washington stood firm in defense of the Government's authority.

He also took opportunities to reinforce his support of the liberties embodied in the Bill of Rights, like his support of religious freedom expressed in a letter to the Touro Synagogue in Newport, Rhode Island. In August of 1790, Washington wrote a brief letter to the Hebrew Congregation that focused on the success of the American experiment in toleration. The letter read in part;

"If we have the wisdom to make the best use of the advantages with which we are now favored, we cannot fail, under the just administration of a good government, to become a great and happy people. The citizens of the United States of America have a right to applaud themselves for having given mankind examples of an enlarged and liberal policy—a policy worthy of imitation. All possess the liberty of conscience and immunities of citizenship. It is now no more that toleration is spoken of as if it were the indulgence of one class of people that another enjoyed the exercise of their inherent natural rights, for, happily, the Government of the United States, which gives to bigotry no sanction, to persecution no assistance requires only that they who live under its protection should demean themselves as good citizens by giving their effectual support on all occasions.

May the children of the stock of Abraham who dwells in this land continue to merit and to enjoy the goodwill of the other inhabitants - while everyone shall sit in safety under his own vine and fig tree, and there shall be none to make him afraid."

"Gives bigotry no sanction, persecution no assistance, a policy for the world to imitate," the words of our first President, one of our founding fathers, praising the values of diversity and tolerance in the new nation, are relevant today. I wonder what he would think about the lack of tolerance in our nation today. His short letter promoted religious tolerance and emphasized the importance of diversity in the new republic. It has been quoted often over the years to emphasize the importance of these basics. It is as relevant today {perhaps even more so} as the day Washington wrote it and should be required reading for American citizens. In writing this short letter, Washington made it clear that the founding fathers of our nation intended to create a system of self-governance that honored diversity. Today, self-anointed 'constitutional experts' should keep this in mind.

He vetoed only two bills in his eight-year term. One of those vetoes dealt with apportionment.

Washington rejected the bill because he felt it did not evenly determine representation, which was contrary to the ideals of democracy. His opposition to what he considered an unfair apportionment demonstrated his strong belief in the authority resting in the electorate, as expressed in a fair election. That authority should not be diluted through disproportional representation. Given this veto, one does not need to wonder how our first President would feel about the current widespread use of Gerrymandering.

As one of the founding fathers and the nation's first president, Washington was a central figure in the creation of the world's greatest democracy. He helped structure it and then set the precedent for its protection. He saw the country's elected officials, including the President, as public servants charged with the temporary responsibility of guiding the nation, no more and no less. They would serve at the pleasure of the people without special privileges. Their authority would come from the consent of the people as expressed at the ballot box. The right of the governed to vote was central to the system, and elections represented the voice of the people. Elections were to be the final arbiter. These principles embodied in our constitution and implemented by our first President are today under attack by those who put their own desire to maintain power above their pledge to honor the constitution.

ABRAHAM LINCOLN

In First Principles, Thomas Ricks states that "the classical knowledge of the founders steered them wrong on the matter of human bondage, which would prove disastrous to the nation they designed." This would be the case as the sixteenth president took office in 1861. He would have to face a nation bitterly divided over 'the peculiar institution'.

The nomination for President of Abraham Lincoln, with his anti-slavery platform, set off the powder keg that had been held at bay for decades by a series of compromises. The peculiar institution had been a divisive issue threatening the Union for fifty years. The southern states that supported slavery could not stand idle as Lincoln took office without the support of a single southern state. Talk of secession, which had been around for decades, became more serious. By the time he was inaugurated, seven states had already seceded as the greatest challenge to the republic took shape. On his first night in office, Fort Sumter, South Carolina, was under siege by the newly formed army of the Confederate States of America. The country was literally splitting in half, creating the greatest challenges for the new president. As he took up occupancy in the White House it seemed war was inevitable.

President Lincoln's cabinet was not unanimous on the matter of going to war to save the Union. Some wished to keep the peace rather than challenge secession. Lincoln believed it to be his sacred duty to preserve the Union. It was this belief, even more than his desire to end slavery, that made war between the states inevitable. Lincoln had made the decision to send ships to resupply Fort Sumter. The southern forces intercepted the ships, ratcheting up the tension. Lincoln said the pending battle was more than a state's rights controversy it was a battle to preserve democracy itself. His election by a majority vote of the people represented democracy in action.

He believed the majority of the country expressed their opposition to slavery by his election, and the will of the majority must prevail. This man who took office during the most divisive, perilous of times was committed to preserving the Union and preserving the democracy upon which the country was founded. As the war raged on, as casualties mounted, one can only imagine the mental anguish Lincoln endured. Did he question his decision? He certainly must have, but he never wavered in his commitment to defend democracy and preserve the union.

Lincoln signed the Emancipation Proclamation on January 1, 1863, but slavery did not officially end until the passage of the thirteenth Amendment. Lincoln steered that Amendment through the House on January 31, 1865, with only two votes to spare. Fighting continued after the passage of the amendment, and so did negotiations.

In a meeting on February 3, 1865, with Confederate representatives aboard the steamer The River Queen, discussions were held in an attempt to end the conflict. Lincoln refused to compromise on the restoration of the Union or on total emancipation, insisting that the will of the majority to end the peculiar institution would prevail and the Union would be preserved. In his second inaugural address a month later, he stated his goal of "a lasting peace among ourselves." He wanted to proceed with reconstruction without bitterness, as he stated in his address, "with malice towards none, charity for all."

The Thirteenth Amendment was ratified by the states in December of 1865 to end slavery. Lincoln was not alive to witness this event. He was not alive to follow through on his objective to heal the nation after the war. His desire to preserve the Union would have guided the nation through the difficult aftermath. His death before he was able to bring the

Union back together was one more tragedy of the times. However, his staunch defense of democracy and his dedication to preserving a nation "of the people, by the people, and for the people" guided our democracy through this greatest of challenges. The nation was divided over the slavery issue, and it took a war to unite it once again. The great efforts of a great President and the objective of all those who made the great sacrifice in the Civil War to hold our country together are today once again in peril.

The United States once again is terribly divided as our democracy and our Union is threatened. Just as in the case of President Washington and the founding fathers, sacred principles of governance are being threatened today. President Lincoln's commitment to preserving the Union and its' democracy is also threatened today. As one presidential campaign in 2024 capitalizes on our differences, and our fears, our nation becomes ever more divided. For the sole purpose of political gain a number of today's 'public servants' seek to capitalize on our divisions.

FRANKLIN DELANO ROOSEVELT

"The measure of my administration's success would not be how we enhance the position of the wealthy, but rather in how we provide for those who have little."

FDR

Like Lincoln, seventy-plus years before him, Franklin Delano Roosevelt took office at a perilous time. The world was struggling with the Great Depression, an economic crisis like no other before. In the United States, unemployment would reach 24.9%, productivity had fallen to one-third of the 1929 levels, and the banking and financial systems had collapsed. The sense that capitalism had failed was making the rise of Communism and Nazism in Europe look more attractive to Americans. Truly, both capitalism and our democratic system were equally in peril in very desperate economic times.

Roosevelt took office with complete confidence that these problems could be addressed. His first one hundred days became legendary as he literally hit the ground running. No President ever took office with the confidence, the determination, and the drive of FDR. Knowing he had to act quickly, he shepherded seventy-seven bills through Congress in his first one hundred days. His first bill, the Emergency Banking Act, passed Congress in one day, only five days after his inauguration. The emergency legislation stabilized the banking industry as a first step toward recovery. Only one copy of the bill was available for the House, so the bill was read into the record before being passed unanimously. A repeal of prohibition followed, and a comprehensive farm bill, plus several bills to stimulate the economy, as Roosevelt took charge of a very troubling situation.

Roosevelt believed that a key to protecting our democracy was to have an economy that worked for everyone. An economy that catered to a small group of wealthy people while leaving behind the masses would result in people losing hope as they struggled to survive, the very situation we see today. America was coming off the "Gilded Age," a time of great wealth disparity. He understood that the greatest threat to Capitalism was wealth, disparity, and the greed that drove it, so his Legislative focus was threefold;

1. To create employment, he launched several infrastructure projects around the nation. He started the Civil Conservation Corps, and established the Tennessee Valley Authority among other infrastructure projects he set in motion to provide employment opportunity.

2. To control the greed in the financial sector that was part of the reason for the Depression, he established the Security and Exchange Commission, passed the Glass Steagall Act, and created the Federal Deposit Insurance Corporation to renew public confidence in the banking industry.

3. To distribute the wealth of the nation more evenly and to create a strong middle-class he raised the top Marginal Income Tax bracket, expanded workers' rights, established the

minimum wage and the Fair Labor Relations Board. To take the elderly out of poverty he established the social security system.

His enemies called him a socialist, but a strong case can be made that he saved capitalism while at the same time saving our democracy. The effects of the New Deal policies were many. Income growth and wealth were shared more evenly, a prosperous, expanding middle class was created, the financial industry was stabilized, workers' rights were expanded, and social security took the elderly out of poverty. The Government paid its bills while having money for infrastructure improvements. All this would come under attack fifty years after FDR's election as a new economy based on 'trickle-down economics' would once again cater to a small wealthy minority as was the case in the 'Gilded Age.'

It is important to review and understand what these three great Presidents did to establish the world's greatest, long-lasting democracy. They faced perilous times but worked to preserve a system in which authority rested with the people through the electoral process. A great system that then needed to be protected and preserved during a Civil War and an economic crisis.

While today, the great majority of Americans continue to revere these three past presidents, a large percentage of the public is completely blind to the dismantling of their legacy. There has never been any guarantee that our democracy will survive. Still, the actions of Presidents Lincoln and Roosevelt show that democracy is a system that is able to deal with difficult times. The problems we now face as a nation and as a world community can also be dealt with by the government established so long ago by our founding fathers.

There is ample evidence that we have already become an oligarchy rather than a democracy. There is a very real danger today that we are on the verge of further transformation into an authoritarian form of Government. Autocracy is the exact antithesis of the ideals upon which our country was founded.

DEMOCRACY

The principles that formed the foundation of our democracy – voting rights, equal representation, and the peaceful transfer of power are all under attack. Even more disturbing, we now have a system in which a small minority exercises the greatest influence, if not the total control of our Government. In addition, we are a nation divided, and the divisions are the greatest they have been since the time of Lincoln. There are those who benefit from and encourage those divisions. The founding principles implemented by Washington and the work of two Presidents to protect our democracy are all under attack today. The country desperately needs a leader that will protect our founding principles while uniting, not dividing us. It does not seem that we have chosen such a leader.

How did we reach this point? When did the transformation begin? Will we be able to reverse the demise of our democracy? The following pages will attempt to answer these questions.

CHAPTER 4

THE THREATS TO DEMOCRACY

Our democratic foundation is under attack on several different fronts. Key elements that have made our form of government work and built our foundation have been chipped away over the past forty years. It is an essential part of our heritage that the right to vote is sacred, that election results are respected as the final arbiter, that the transfer of power is done peacefully, and that no single group has an undue influence on the electoral process. All these essential elements of democracy have been severely challenged if not completely crippled over the past forty years.

DEMOCRACY

The re-election of Donald Trump to a second term threatens to continue the attack on democracy. Love him or hate him {there is no in-between} one must give him credit for a remarkable comeback. While giving credit for the return one must also recognize a degree of luck that has been involved. There are at least three events that would have killed the return effort that luckily for the Trump team never fell into place:

- After the attack on the Capital instigated by the outgoing President the House voted to impeach him even after he had left office. A conviction by the Senate would have barred Trump from ever holding office again. Even after running for their lives from his invading supporters Republicans in the Senate could not muster the courage to vote to convict. Only seven Republicans joined with the fifty Democrats causing the vote to fall three votes short.

- Newly elected President Joe Biden chose as his Attorney General the very weak Merrick Garland who chose to prosecute the thugs who invaded the Capital in an attempt to prevent the certification of the election. The millions of dollars in damage to the 'people's building', the beating of police officers and the defecating in the halls of Congress certainly deserved to be prosecuted, but he took no action against the organizers of the assault including Trump. It was not until the work of the 'January sixth committee' forced him to take action that he appointed a special prosecutor to deal with the organizers. Waiting so long allowed Trump, an expert in finding ways to delay justice, {with the help of the corrupt judiciary} to put off any trials until after election day. His winning of the election means he will avoid any consequences for his actions.

- President Biden's age became an issue early on in the 2024 campaign. A pathetic performance in a debate against Trump made it obvious to all that he was failing to the point that his ability to serve four more years was in doubt. His decision to withdraw should have come long before it did allowing for a primary to determine his Democratic successor. Even if Vice President Kamala Harris had ended up as the nominee the primary would have given voters a better chance to get to know her and feel comfortable with her as President. The election results may have been different if President Biden had acted earlier.

Donald Trump and his MAGA followers have been successful in casting doubts amongst many Americans about our electoral process, our judiciary, our Department of Justice, and our law enforcement agencies. The result has been a lack of trust in the very institutions that provide the checks and balances that were such an important part of the work of our founding fathers in designing our system of Government. The rule of law and the electoral process have been cast in doubt for many citizens by a series of lies and conspiracy theories. The idea that an election can be stolen by nefarious means in the United States has taken root due to one man not being able to accept defeat. Now that one man is headed back to the White House. The resulting harm to our country may not be possible to fix.

VOTING RIGHTS

Arguably the most important civil rights legislation ever enacted, the Voting Rights Act of 1965, prohibited states from imposing qualifications to deny racial minorities the right to vote. Further, it provided for direct federal intervention in the electoral process to protect these rights in certain states with a history of voter restrictions. The law required preclearance by the Justice Department for any new voting laws in those same states.

The act has been re-authorized and/or amended five times in 1970, 1975, 1982, 1992, and 2006 by large, bipartisan majorities in both Houses of Congress. There was strong support for voting rights in both major political parties until most recently when one party decided it was to their political advantage to restrict voter access. Declining support for the Republican Party amongst minority groups, coupled with the growth in population within those same minorities, inspired the declining support for voting rights within the Republican Party.

The 1982 reauthorization of the Voting Rights Act was unsuccessfully opposed by some members of the legal staff within the Reagan White House. In 2005, President George W. Bush appointed one of the leading opponents in the Reagan White House of the 1982 reauthorization to serve as Chief Justice of the Supreme Court. John Roberts assumed that position on September 29, 2005, giving him a seat of power from which to continue his opposition to the Voting Rights Act and, indeed, to the act of voting itself. Since his appointment he has been on a crusade to lead the court to take actions to restrict voting.

Chief Justice Roberts had the prime opportunity to weaken the Voting Rights Act in the case of Shelby County vs Holder in 2013. In a five-to-four vote on the Supreme Court, the very key section 5 of the act was stripped out. Section five was the section that required states with a history of racial discrimination to get the justice department's approval for any changes to their voting laws. The majority opinion written by Roberts basically declared the section no longer relevant. In her minority opinion, Ruth Bader Ginsburg wrote, "Throwing out preclearance when it has worked and is continuing to work to stop discriminatory changes is like throwing away your umbrella in a rainstorm because you are not getting wet."

The Court's ruling severely limited the ability of the Justice Department's Civil Rights Division to do its job in the area of voting rights. Basically it opened the door for a flood of voter restrictions in a number of states to suit the objective of limiting the minority vote totals. With the Trump transition team's recent recommendation that long time Trump supporter, Harmeet Dhillon should head the Civil Rights Division, we can expect total support within the Department for more efforts to restrict voting rights over the next four years.

It did not take long after this Court ruling for states to take advantage of the opportunity. It was no longer necessary to have changes in voting laws approved by the Justice Department. The conservative judges on the court had done their job opening the door for voting restrictions. It was now open season for voter restrictions. The measures enacted to restrict voting rights took several forms, including:

- Closing polling places. Often, these closings targeted areas populated by people of color. The result has been long lines and long waits at the polling places that are left open in these districts. The long lines were intended to discourage voting in districts selected because of their voting history. During the 2024 elections the long lines were thinned out by use of a nationwide series of bomb threats at selected polling places. The threats were intended to discourage voting in these key districts and there can be little doubt that they were effective.

- Voter identification cards – in some states, efforts were made to make these special IDs difficult to obtain for people lacking transportation and/or computer skills. Voter ID laws that intentionally made acquisitions difficult often specifically targeted minority groups. "The overwhelming evidence reflects that there are hundreds of thousands of qualified voters who lack compliant ID." Those are the words of the Pennsylvania Commonwealth Court, which struck down one such law. Similar court challenges in other states have resulted in the courts reaching the conclusion that the laws were racially motivated.

- Purging of voter rolls – again aimed at affecting voters with unfriendly party affiliation.

A study by the Leadership Conference Education Fund conducted in 2016 after the Shelby County v Holder decision identified 868 polling place closures in states formerly covered by section 5 of the Voting Rights Act. A later report, Democracy Diverted:

Polling Place Closures and the Right to Vote found 1,688 closures between 2012 and 2018 roughly double the 2016 report. States like Texas, Arizona, and Georgia, with heavy African American and Latino populations, led the way with poll closings, 750 in Texas alone. A 2019 report in Reuters identified seven counties in Georgia with only one polling place, as well as identifying Republican-led states imposing a range of restrictions, including shorter voting hours. These restrictions have had a disproportionate impact on groups unlikely to vote Republican.

Voter identification laws of some kind have been enacted in thirty-six states. Some states' laws are more restrictive than others. In North Carolina, the omnibus restrictive election law, which included voter ID, was struck down when the Fourth Circuit Court ruled it was purposefully racially discriminatory. These laws, along with the purging of voter lists, have been justified as attempts to protect our system of voting from fraud. However, studies indicate that these efforts to address fraud in our electoral process are all a solution in search of a problem.

Many studies over the years have reached the same conclusion basically that widespread voter fraud does not exist. The Brennan Center's Report, 'The Truth about Voter Fraud,' found incident rates of fraud between 0.0003 percent and 0.00.25 percent. Two studies by Arizona State University – one in 2012 and another in 2016 – found only ten cases of voter impersonation fraud nationwide from 2000 to 2012. A 2014 study by the non-partisan government accountability office reviewed a number of studies, concluding they 'constantly found few instances of fraud.' A 2011 study by the Republican National Lawyers Association found that between 2000 and 2010, twenty-one states had 1 or 0 convictions of voter fraud. The list can go on and on, but suffice to say that no legitimate studies have ever found widespread voter fraud of a degree that could change election results in the United States.

Michael Waldron's, The Briefing, reported that all these voter restriction efforts have combined to increase the white/black voter turnout gap between nine and twenty-one percentage points across five of the six states originally covered by section five of the Voting Rights Act. There is an abundance of evidence that people of color vote democrat by over whelming majorities, so it is no accident that these actions initiated in states with Republican Party control widened the turn out gap, it has been the objective. The efforts at voter restrictions are obviously contrary to the beliefs of our founding fathers and the compliance, and support for these efforts by the highest court in America is an absolute disgrace.

With Section 5 of the Voting Rights Act gone, voting rights groups turned to Section two of the same act, which allows them to sue after the fact to prove discriminatory voting practices. A number of successful challenges under section 2 resulted in the 2021 case of Brovich vs. Democratic National Committee. The Supreme Court ruling on this case made it much harder to use section two against discriminatory voting laws as Chief Justice

Roberts continued his crusade to make voting a more difficult task in America.

The attacks on the Voting Rights Act continue to this day, as a very recent ruling by the Eighth Circuit Court of Appeals marks a further restriction in the enforcement of the law using section two. For decades, civil rights groups like the NAACP and the American Civil Liberty Union had filed suits under section two when it was felt voting rights were being abused by redistricting or by ID requirements. The two-to-one decision by the Eighth Circuit Appeals Court upheld a lower court ruling that private citizens and civil rights groups cannot sue under the act. The ruling that private plaintiffs have no standing leaves enforcement power solely with the Attorney General of the United States. When the office of Attorney General is occupied by a disciple of the restrictions, as will be the case in the Trump administration, there will be no actions taken under section two. The ruling will certainly be appealed to the Supreme Court, but given the record on voting rights of the Robert's Court, this ruling will likely be upheld, further gutting the most important civil rights act ever passed.

The idea of limiting the voter turnout for a specific group in order to win elections would have never taken root in the Republican Party of Dwight Eisenhower. The acceptance of this outrageously undemocratic way to win an election is just one of the astounding 'new principles' of the modern Republican Party. It stands has an example of the far reaching Republican Party planning to gain and keep power by undemocratic means.

GERRYMANDERING

Gerrymandering is not a new practice. It has been happening in America for centuries. In fact, the term dates back to 1812, when the Governor of Massachusetts, Eldridge Gerry, signed a bill creating a partisan district in Boston in the shape of a salamander, hence the name gerrymandering. While the practice is not new, it has always been considered a corruption of the democratic process.

It is a practice that has reached new levels in recent years as both parties strive to create 'safe districts'.

Basically, Gerrymandering is the political manipulation of electoral districts to create an advantage for one political party. It can come in two forms. One method is referred to as "cracking," whereby the voting power of one party's base is diluted by spreading that parties voters out to several districts. "Packing" is the opposite method, whereby district lines are drawn in a way that concentrates one party's core voters into one district. The result of both methods is to create "safe" districts for one party's candidates by basically having the political candidate pick his or her voters rather than the voters picking the politician. The creation of 'safe districts' has the obvious effect of limiting the number of competitive districts. With fewer competitive districts it becomes easier to promote party loyalty. Lack of party loyalty can result in a primary and in a safe district that becomes a bigger worry than a general election opponent.

Gerrymandering is effective because it creates a 'wasted vote' effect whereby votes are cast that do not contribute to electing a candidate because the district has been overloaded with voters favoring one party. District lines are redrawn after every census by political figures that usually hold an office in the state legislature. Basically the lines are redrawn by politicians. When drawing district lines, the party in power concentrates the opposition voters into a few districts they would already win, which wastes the excess votes of the minority party. Other district lines are then drawn to intentionally leave the opposition party in a small minority thereby creating a safe district. This generally works to the advantage of the incumbent, leaving little chance it will be changed because officeholders will not vote to change a system in which they are benefitting. Gerrymandering has always been a corruption in the democratic process. Remember that one of the two vetoes by President Washington involved unfair voting districts. As early as the administration of our first president the practice of gerrymandering was seen as corrupt.

The end result of Gerrymandering is that thousands of votes cast across the country in congressional races are ineffective either because their vote is part of a super majority because of packing or a tiny minority because of cracking. This is a predictable outcome when the task of drawing district lines is left in the hands of sitting politicians. The main objective of the politicians drawing the lines will be to create safe districts for their parties candidates. Because both political parties want their share of 'safe districts, ' one hand will wash the other, eliminating any protests.

Today, there are ample examples of the practice used by both political parties. Some of the more blatant examples;

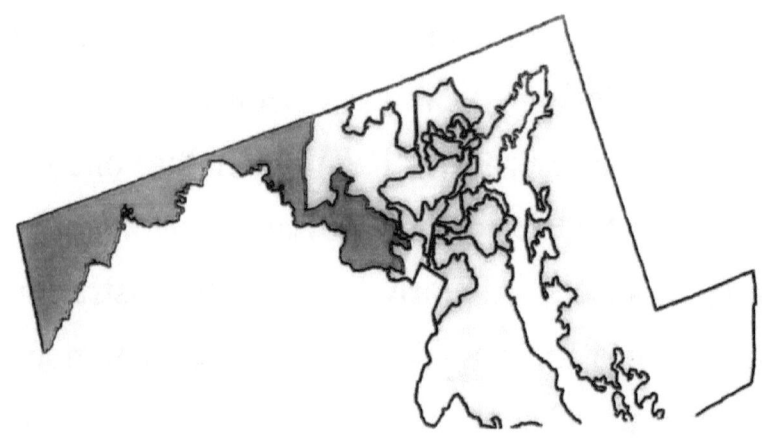

DEMOCRACY

Maryland's sixth Congressional District was involved in the Supreme Court decision in the case of Rucho et al. Vs. Common Cause et al. The Court ruled in that case that Federal Courts have no jurisdiction over partisan Gerrymandering. Voters in North Carolina and Maryland filed a lawsuit challenging the districting maps as unconstitutional, partisan Gerrymandering. Even as the Democrats in control of the mapping admitted that the lines of the district were drawn to dilute Republican voting strength, the Court refused to get involved. The 5 to 4 decision was yet another blow to democracy by the Roberts Court. Politicians would never act to end the practice so the only avenue for redress was closed off by this decision.

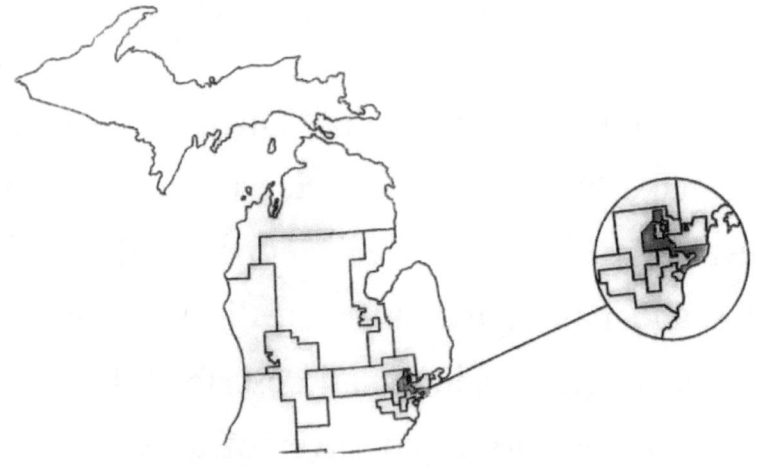

Michigan's 14th Congressional District results from the Republican Party's control of the forming of the house map. It combines heavily black populated areas in Pontiac and Detroit, 31 miles apart. The obvious goal of the Republican map makers is to put as many minority voters who are prone to vote Democrat into one district to minimize their impact.

Ohio's ninth Congressional District, known as the 'snake by the lake' stretches from Toledo to Cleveland, squeezing in an overload of democratic votes, and making it a super safe district. A panel of Federal Judges in Cincinnati described the district as "a bizarre, elongated sliver of a district" and "blatant partisan gerrymandering." Despite this definition there is no federal remedy because of the Supreme Court ruling that partisan redistricting is a political question that is not reviewable by federal courts.

The courts are the only forum for reform as the legislators responsible for drawing the maps were unlikely to take action. The courts' abdication allows a practice to continue that may cause irreparable damage to our system of Government. The Supreme Court ruling basically sets the precedent that the judicial system would prefer to avoid the question than to correct the very undemocratic practice.

There have been several proposals to address Gerrymandering in countries around the world. In the U.S., any change must maintain the one-man, one-vote rule. Perhaps the simplest solution is to take redistricting away from the legislature and have it done by a non-partisan panel appointed by the state's Supreme Court coupled with a set of precise criteria established by the court. This would theoretically take politics out of the system of drawing district lines. However, trying to accomplish this type of change would meet with resistance from both major parties because they both benefit from the status quo.

THE PEACEFUL TRANSFER OF POWER

There is no provision more necessary for the preservation of democracy than accepting the will of the voters. Our founding fathers made it very clear that the power of the government depended on the consent of the governed. That consent was provided by the electoral process and the result of the elections would always be the final arbiter. After the 2020 Presidential election, the nation experienced for the first time a President refusing to peacefully yield the power of the office after losing an election. Even after being told by his closest advisers that he had lost in a clean, fair election, even after being advised that there was no widespread fraud that would have changed the result, even after his own appointment to head cyber security, Chris Kreb, called it the

DEMOCRACY

cleanest election in history, Donald Trump refused to concede. He claimed, without offering any proof, that the election was stolen.

Ample evidence has surfaced that leaves no doubt that Trump knew he lost, yet he refused and still refuses to admit his defeat. Rather, he claimed the election had been stolen from him by means of 'widespread fraud." It is important to note that countless court cases and recounts in a number of states have found no incidents of widespread fraud. He and his people went to incredible lengths to hold onto the power of the Presidency, despite his loss, including:

- Multiple unsuccessful court cases. The Supreme Court ruling in the 2000 election had installed George W. Bush as our first 'court-appointed President.' One could argue that the Trump administration, after seeing this, could be justified in turning to the courts. However, courts still require proof, so the appeals without evidence fell upon deaf ears so the Trump team went beyond appeals to the judicial branch.

- Bullying state officials in key battleground states to get them to claim the election was fraudulent – again unsuccessfully.

- Illegally putting together lists of fake electors to compete with the electors chosen by the voters.

- Even considering having the military seize voting machines.

- Pressuring the justice department to claim that there was widespread fraud even as top officials in the department told him there was not.

- Finally, organizing a rally to promote a storming of the Capitol to intimidate Congress and the Vice President into not certifying the election.

As foreign as this attempted coup was to our centuries-old democracy, the insane part of it all was the support it received from not only the group that stormed the Capital but from Republican members of Congress. Many of these same members who ran, in fear for their lives, from the Trump supporters who stormed the Capital later voted to not certify the election. Even after experiencing the criminal attack, Republicans then went into session and voted against certifying the results. Many House and Senate members who refused to certify the results of the presidential election were themselves re-elected in the same electoral process, on the same ballots. Yet they cling to the lie about widespread election fraud. Apparently, they believe the 'fraud' that stole the election from Trump was not an issue in their races decided on the same ballot. What is even more disturbing is that a significant minority in the general public still believe the election was stolen. They seem to accept the attempted coup to turn over the legitimate results as a justifiable act by the co-conspirators. In his successful campaign to reclaim the White House, Trump promised to pardon the thugs who stormed the capitol. In spite of witnessing with their own eyes the desecration of the 'people's building' voters were fine with this promise.

Despite a complete lack of any evidence to support the claim of fraud, despite a series of illegal, unconstitutional acts, a large number of citizens continue to believe the claim of a stolen election based solely on the word of Trump and a small group of sycophants. Even after all the illegal attempts to hold onto an office he lost voters returned Trump to the Presidency still believing the lie. The fact that members of Congress, as well as several conservative 'news outlets,' still support Trump in his claim is a large part of the reason for the public support.

The purpose of discussing this here is not to go into details of what happened in the attempted coup. There will be dozens of books written that will detail the attempted coup better than I. Rather, the purpose of this book is to attempt to analyze the long-term effect of these actions on our democracy.

One hundred and forty-seven House Republicans and six senators, all Republicans, voted against certifying the election. In 1861, eleven senators and three house members were removed from office for refusing to recognize that Abraham Lincoln had been duly elected. As of this writing, no action has been taken against the one hundred and fifty-three treasonous officeholders who acted the same way as the Lincoln deniers. If today's Congress had the courage and high moral standards to police themselves the 153 Biden deniers would suffer the same fate as the Lincoln deniers. Treason in 1861 is still treason in 2021. The lack of any action to hold these congressional election deniers accountable for their actions is another way in which the 'big lie' has become plausible for many Americans.

Immediate action should have been taken following the attempted coup. The inaction of the very weak Attorney General has resulted in the entire affair being swept away by time. Given the result of the 2024 election no action will ever be taken against these congressional election deniers. Nor will any action be taken against Trump and his fellow conspirators who organized the coup. This lack of accountability coupled with the pardoning of the convicted rioters who caused millions of dollars of damage to our Capitol, defecated and urinated in the halls, beat police officers causing four deaths, will all be a great example for the youth of America. The precedent set by the lack of criminal charges against President Nixon has now been reaffirmed in the nation that use to be able to claim that no one is above the law.

To be sure, there have been elections in our history that were much closer and had more reason to suspect fraud than the 2020 election. Most recently, the 1960 election of John F. Kennedy and the 2000 election of George W. Bush are good examples. In both cases, there were questions asked about voting in one key state. In the 1960 election, it was Illinois, in 2000 it was Florida.

In both cases, the losing candidate conceded the election for the good of the country. No such magnanimous gesture was to come from Trump, even as his defeat was by a far wider margin than was the case for Nixon and Gore. His despicable actions that continue to this day constitute a blueprint for transitioning to an authoritarian state in which election results are of no consequence. If enough of the American public can be convinced that election results are suspect, then losing candidates can repeat the efforts to hold on to power with the support of those who have come to not trust election results. Essentially, elections will no longer matter. After voters ignored his actions following the 2020 election, and voted him back into office in 2024 there were no claims of fraud. This was the case because the losing candidate, Vice President Harris, accepted the results. There is little doubt that the fraud claims would have been made again had Trump lost the election.

The reason the voting in Illinois in 1960 and in Florida in 2000 were so important to the result of the Presidential election was solely because of the very undemocratic practice of having the Electoral College determine the winner rather than the popular vote. In the past twenty-five years, the

United States Presidency has been won by two men who lost the popular vote. That fact alone represents a bastardization of democracy. The Electoral College is a system in which the President and Vice President are chosen by electors from each state, not by the popular vote of the people. At the time of the Philadelphia convention, no other country in the world directly elected its chief executive. This, coupled with the inherent distrust amongst the founders of executive power, inspired a lively debate between those who felt the Congress should pick the president and those who felt the office should be filled by popular vote. The Electoral College became the compromise, and today, it stands as an undemocratic, outdated institution that has outlived its usefulness and should be eliminated.

Added to the peculiar process of picking a president, we have now had the first instance of a losing incumbent refusing to accept his defeat while doing all he can to hold on to power by illegal means. This refusal to participate in the peaceful transfer of power has resulted in two major blows to the democratic system that Americans have fought and died to protect.

First, we now have other losing candidates following Trump's lead by refusing to accept the results of an election they lost. In the 2020 election in Arizona, Republican Gubernatorial candidate Kari Lake refused to concede after a losing effort, claiming the election was stolen. In the same election, the Republican candidate for Secretary of State, Mark Finchman, made the same claim after losing. In both cases, the losing candidates made no effort to provide any evidence to support their claim. Like Trump, they merely stated the claim as fact while providing no supporting evidence.

In Nevada, Gubernatorial candidate Joey Gilbert paid for a recount even though he lost by 11 points. Again, without any evidence, he claimed there were irregularities and refused to concede.

In Florida, Jason Mariner lost a special election by a whopping 59 percentage points then filed a lawsuit claiming inconsistencies in the system. His statement in filing the lawsuit is telling, "They say I did not win but that does not mean we lost".

As absurd as these cases may be, these types of conspiracy theories and denials only serve to further erode people's confidence in our electoral system. Sadly, it also seems to be the way of the future. We will see more losing candidates refuse to concede defeat while making wild claims of stolen elections, and that provides the next blow to our democracy.

The second blow to democracy is that it has resulted in a portion of the electorate distrusting the results of our elections without any evidence to support their skepticism. Election deniers in the GOP, as well as in conservative media, continue to claim the 2020 presidential election was stolen, although not one piece of evidence has ever emerged to back the claim. Donald Trump made the claim after being told by his Attorney General and his White House Attorney, amongst countless others, that it was false. Evidence emerges weekly that Trump understood he lost the election. He and none of his fellow deniers have ever offered evidence to back the claim, yet like Lemmings, a core group of his followers continue to believe the lie. Even worse, Republicans are using the distrust in elections, distrust that they created with this lie, to enact even more voter restrictions. Voter fraud is a farcical claim being used now to promote the destruction of democracy.

In early 2021, shortly after the insurrection at the Capital, states began passing comprehensive voter restriction laws with the claim that they were enhancing the integrity of the electoral process. These are the same people whose support of the lie and conspiracy claims, are destroying the integrity of the process. Georgia passed a law that reduced the time to request absentee ballots while requiring new demands on voters making the request. Absentee ballots could only be approved under the new law after the applicant provided voter ID, the last four digits of their social security number plus proof of residence. Drop boxes were restricted in number, with a requirement for a minimum number of registered voters per box. In the heavily Democratic greater Atlanta area, the law reduced the number of drop boxes from 94 to 23. The law also gave greater control over election administration to the Georgia General Assembly and even made it a crime to provide water to voters waiting in line for an extended period to cast their ballot. Major League Baseball found the law so repugnant that they moved the 2021 All-Star Game out of Atlanta. The outrage generated by the law's original passage has now subsided to the point of acceptance, which has encouraged other states to pass similar laws.

Other states followed including, Texas and Florida who were close behind, with similar law changes soon to be emulated by most red states. It did not stop in 2021. It has continued with the Brennan Center for Justice, sighting 45 state legislatures introducing at least 322 bills to restrict democracy.

A proposed bill in the blue state of New York would require first-time voters to provide proof of citizenship when registering. In Nebraska, a proposal would require specific forms of voter ID issued by the State or Federal Government that must be sixty or more days from expiration. Virginia saw a proposal to allow citizens to initiate forensic audits of election results.

The list goes on and on from state to state, where the proposals are offered to 'restore public confidence' in elections. The ironic fact is that the lack of public confidence has been created by the lies of the very Republicans who offer these proposals. The real reason for these proposals is to restrict voting access. It is beyond the scope of this book to examine the effect of all these changes on the 2024 election. However, it is interesting to note that there were roughly three and a half million less votes cast for president in 2024 compared to 2020. Trump's total in 2024 was slightly higher than in 2020, while Harris recorded over six million less votes than Biden in 2020. Across the country it was a story of Democrats losing votes. Of the forty seven counties that Trump won in 2024, and Biden previously won, thirty one were because of a drop in Democratic votes. The various law changes coupled with bomb threats in selected polling places, and the burning of drop boxes may have had a lot to do with the Democratic vote drop. The growth in the numbers of minority groups that are more likely to vote Democrat than Republican is the reason for the growth in voter restrictions. The analysis on the drop in votes for democrats, as well as the drop in votes cast by minorities in 2024 I will leave to others.

A Pew Institute study concluded that rich people are more likely to vote than poor people, and they are more likely to vote Republican. There is also evidence that in the 2024 election Republican candidates improved their support amongst minority voters. Even with that factored in, Republicans fear the numbers, given the growth of minority groups. That being the case we can expect more creative attempts to restrict voting for minority groups in the future. Whatever actions are taken in this regard will have the full support of the Roberts Court.

An even more sinister objective to the voting restriction laws that have passed is detailed in the most recent report from Protect Democracy, 'A DEMOCRACY CRISES IN THE MAKING.' In this study, which was made in partnership with the United Democracy Center and Law Forward and issued in June 2023, concludes that the goal has been to lay the groundwork to enable the election subversion that was unsuccessfully attempted in 2020. The disturbing findings in this report are best described in the research paper summary, which reads in part:

"The third volume of A Democracy Crises in the Making provides a detailed analysis of the nationwide trend of State Legislatures considering laws that increase the risk of election subversion and its potential impact on election administration in the 2024 elections. The report identifies 185 bills in 38 states that would make it easier to manipulate an election, with 15 of them becoming law as of May 3, 2023. This is on top of nearly 400 election subversion bills identified in previous reports that were introduced in 2021 and 2022, with 56 of those becoming law in 26 states.

The legislative trends have recently intensified, with bills around the country passing or advancing. Partisan state legislatures are trying to seize control over election administration, taking it away from trusted local election officials. As of a December 2021 update, 262 bills have been introduced in 41 states that would interfere with election administration—and 32 have become law across 17 states. As of our August 2022 update, 244 bills have been introduced in 33 states, including in Wisconsin, that allow state legislatures to politicize, criminalize, or interfere with elections. The 2020 election is over, but attempts to undermine our democracy are not. These threats can't be ignored."

These efforts to subvert our electoral process and transfer the authority to decide elections away from the voters should be met with outrage from the American public, yet there is little opposition expressed. The lack of opposition by the general public is disturbing, but the silence of public officials who see this happening is more disturbing. Every day, evidence comes to light in the various legal proceedings ongoing that Trump and his entourage all knew full well that he had lost in the fair election. They all knew there was no 'mass fraud,' no 'irregularities,' yet they continued to spew the big lie. On the strength of that lie, they have attacked voting rights, and the unfolding evidence of the lie has not slowed the efforts. The question that needs to be thoroughly examined is how much effect these law changes had on the 2024 election. In addition, as these efforts continue what will be the effect in future elections? Has elected officials in both parties, who took seriously their oath to defend the Constitution, sit numbly by watching this all unfold it does not inspire confidence in our future as a democracy.

The efforts of Republican law makers are so aggressive that the party of "state's rights" has even abandoned that former Republican Party principle. Election laws have been generally the province of the states throughout our history. Notwithstanding that tradition, congressional Republicans have proposed the American Confidence in Elections Act at the federal level. Apparently not satisfied with the efforts at the state level to restrict voting this bill proposes to nationalize the same onerous restrictions on voting rights. It would impose national voter ID for mail-in ballots while cutting federal funds to states that allow community organizations to assist voters in returning ballots. Amongst other provisions, it also further loosens controls on the dark money fed into our political system.

The Leadership Conference on Civil and Human Rights authored a letter signed by 45 other organizations protesting this undemocratic proposal. It seems there are no limits to how low the Republican Party will stoop to restrict voting rights. The party has become convinced that the more they can extend restrictions to people's right to vote, the easier it will be for them to gain and hold power. If the results of the 2024 election are any indication, they may be right.

Members of the GOP along with the majority of the general public continue to support Trump, knowing his fraud claim is a lie that is causing damage to our democracy. What's more, the lack of support for the integrity of our electoral process flies in the face of reality. As cited earlier, study after study over the years have all reached the conclusion that voter fraud in America is rare and our electoral system is free and fair.

In a desperate attempt to prove all the studies wrong, Trump signed an executive order in May 2017 establishing the Presidential Advisory Commission on Election Integrity. He appointed his Vice president, Mike Pence, as the chair and Kansas Secretary of State Kris Kobach as vice chair.

Trump made sure he had a friendly face in charge, as Kobach was a longtime supporter of basically every conspiracy theory around election fraud. So, the table was set. However, a problem arose when they also appointed a democratic Secretary of State, Matt Dunlap of Maine, in an attempt to appear bipartisan. There was an early disagreement between Dunlap and Kobach, best described in Dunlap's own words:

"The commission only met in person twice. The first meeting was just an organizational meeting in Washington, D.C., on July 19, 2017. It was in no way substantive. The second meeting was held at Saint Anselm College in New Hampshire. The week before that meeting, Kobach published an opinion piece in the online conservative magazine Breitbart News stating that six thousand voters registered on Election Day in New Hampshire had not changed the address on their driver's license nine months after the election. To him, this was all the proof needed to show that voter fraud existed. My response was a bit more strident, "Making the equation that not updating a driver's license is tantamount to voter fraud is like saying having cash in your wallet is proof that you've robbed a bank."

After this altercation, Dunlap was frozen out of the process, no longer receiving any information or meeting notices. Repeated phone calls and emails to the vice chair were unanswered. A formal letter dated October 17, 2017, finally drew a response from Andrew Kossack of the commission's executive office stating Dunlap's request for information in the possession of the committee, a committee on which Dunlap served, was being reviewed by legal counsel. Eventually, Dunlap filed a lawsuit, and the Washington D.C. District Court granted a preliminary injunction telling the commission to "turn over all working papers to Dunlap and his attorneys." What he found in reviewing the documents is again best told in his own words. "The one document that came into our possession and should frighten every American was the framework for an extensive report on voter fraud. This after only two meetings and virtually no evidence presented, obviously a predetermined result to empower further voter suppression efforts."

The purpose for the creation of this committee was to provide a basis for new voter restrictions. As Dunlap pointed out, the pre-arranged findings were to be used as proof that the restrictions were necessary. The report was never issued. However, a new basis for restrictions was made available with the 'big lie' that the 2020 election was stolen. That lie has been used over the past four years as the proof the unissued Kobach report failed to provide that voter restrictions were necessary. Ironically, the 'lie' that is used as proof never was proven.

The violence of January 6, 2021, was inspired by Trump's claim in his speech to the rally that the election had been stolen and they must "go to the capital and fight like hell. If you don't, you will no longer have a country." All of these events may well be a preview of our future. The attempted coup failed, but it provided a blueprint for a future coup attempt. If steps are not taken to address the actions of the team of conspirators and address the weaknesses in our system, the attempt's after the 2020 election will surely be refined and will happen again.

CHAPTER 5

THE MAKING OF AN OLIGARCHY

"The Government, which was designed for the people, has gone into the hands of the bosses and the special interests. The invisible empire has been set up above the forms of democracy."

President Woodrow Wilson.

This statement from President Wilson was made when the nation was in the throes of the Gilded Age. It was a time of tremendous wealth disparity, a time when those who held the nation's wealth exercised an unhealthy influence on the direction of the country. As accurate as Wilson's observation was at the time, it is just as appropriate today, perhaps even more so, as we once again find ourselves in a state of tremendous economic inequality and disproportionate influence on lawmakers by a wealthy, privileged class. Studies have shown that the wealth and income gap in America today is at a level not seen since the Gilded Age.

How does a democracy become an oligarchy, and has the United States made that transition? How could democracy in the United States, our cherished form of Government for over two hundred years, become a system so foreign to the ideals of our founders? How could democracy decline in a nation where thousands have given their lives to sustain it? The answer is that it happened so gradually that the effects of the subtle changes escaped the attention of much of the general public. In fact, the long-term, dramatic effects of the early actions were not even anticipated by the architects of the changes.

The Reagan administration began the process by lowering the top marginal tax rates for the wealthy, attacking unions and worker's rights, and making regulatory changes for the financial industry that worked in favor of those with great wealth. His entire 'trickle-down' economy had the effect of shifting wealth from the lower 90% to the upper 10% of the richest Americans. The process Reagan started became a runaway train with the subsequent policies of Clinton, George W Bush, and Trump. The Bush and Trump tax cuts, benefiting the wealthy, were reactions to the popularity of President Reagan after his own cuts. The fact that the benefits were channeled to the richest Americans seemed acceptable to the lower 90% who had bought into the trickle down concept. The tremendous wealth and income gap that has resulted would shock even the Reagan team that started the process. Sometimes one needs to be careful what they wish for.

An oligarchy is defined as a small group having control of a country, organization, or institution. An important step in gaining that control within a nation is to restrict voting rights to gain some control over which people can participate in the process, as discussed in the previous chapter. By selectively limiting the number of citizens that can participate in the process you can reduce the number that needs to be managed while at the same time eliminating some of those who are more difficult to manage. The tools of suicide for our democracy in America today are greed and power. To meet the definition of an oligarchy, a small, powerful group would need to be created and then given the tools by which the group can exercise control. That is exactly what has happened in America over the last forty years.

To fully understand the change that has taken place, one has to go back to the Franklin Roosevelt years. His New Deal policies addressed the wealth and income disparity created during the Gilded Age. As referenced in the Woodrow Wilson quote, wealth and the influence of the wealthy had grown to dangerous levels before Roosevelt took office. To address the situation, FDR created a strong middle class capable of active participation in the democratic process. Following his death, his successors – Truman, Eisenhower, Kennedy all the way to Carter continued the support of the middle class. When Eisenhower took office, the first Republican in twenty years, the top marginal income tax rate stood at 90%. Resisting the pressure from within his party, Ike never lowered the rate as he built the interstate highway system without running up the national debt. Roosevelt had built an economy from the bottom up that lasted for fifty years until Ronald Reagan took office. By the late 70s, the Republican Party had been taken over by a philosophy totally foreign to the party that elected Eisenhower. The Johnson administration's 'Great Society' had provided an opportunity for conservatives to make the case that FDR's 'hand up' policies had been transformed into a 'hand out' welfare state by Johnson. Conservatives, using the Johnson agenda, were successful in convincing working glass Americans that their taxes were being used to support 'free loaders'. The case was successfully made that working men and women were being overly taxed to support this welfare state.

The new Republicans were dedicated to restoring the wealth gap FDR had reduced, and they now had the tools to create a political message that would sell. Just as the attacks on voting rights represent a direct effort to undermine the work of Washington and our other founders, these new Republicans would work to undo the work of Roosevelt. They chose as their figurehead to push the changes they desired a former actor who possessed great charisma and the ability to articulate their new message in a way that appealed to America.

The Reagan administration introduced the nation to trickle-down economics, a top-down approach that left the middle class behind while catering to the wealthy. The tax cuts at the top also brought about the beginning of building a national debt the nation may never dissolve as his administration doubled the national debt in a few short years. The plan was to reduce federal revenue with extravagant tax cuts which would force reductions in spending. The result was that Republicans were just as incapable of reducing spending as were their Democratic colleagues. Both sides quickly became convinced that it was easier to run up deficits than to reduce spending.

The administrations that followed Reagan continued to add debt, with the Trump team breaking all records by adding over seven trillion in just four years. It was the exact opposite of the New Deal's approach to building an economy that worked for the benefit of the masses while raising enough revenue to pay our bills, and provide for infrastructure investment.

The Reagan administration began the process of building an economy that created a privileged, wealthy class at the top once again while stagnating the economic well-being of 90% of the people in America. The promise that lower taxes on the wealthy would be a benefit to everyone was a lie. The bottom 90% of Americans are working harder while getting nowhere, and forty years after Reagan, the wealth and income gap has been fully restored. In the economy created by the New Deal, it could accurately be said that the rising tide lifted all boats. In the 'trickle down' economy, the only boats being raised were yachts.

To distribute wealth and opportunity more evenly and create and build a strong middle class, Roosevelt raised taxes on the wealthy, promoted labor unions while expanding job opportunities, created the National Labor Relations Board, and established the minimum wage. When Reagan took office in 1981, the top marginal tax rate on wealthy taxpayers was 73%. When he left in 1989, he had brought it down to 28%, the lowest level since 1925. Whenever it is suggested that the wealthy should pay more in taxes, that idea is termed as 'class warfare' by today's Republicans. When you look at what is funded by taxes at all levels of Government, the services provided benefit the wealthy far more than anyone else. Taxes fund police protection, fire protection, public works, education, infrastructure investment, and national defense. A person making $30,000 a year, renting an apartment, whose only assets are a modest amount of clothing and furniture has little to lose if these services are not provided. On the other hand, a wealthy person or corporation with millions in real estate holdings, plus millions more in stocks, bonds, treasury notes, etc., has a lot at risk without those services. It is only fair that those with the most need for the services should pay more for the protection of their assets. A progressive income tax requires those with the most at risk, those with the greatest ability to pay, will pay their fair share. The tax policies of the Reagan administration did away with the progressive tax brackets.

Reagan attacked unions and fair labor practices. When he was elected, the percentage of workers who belonged to unions was 23.3%. When he left office, it had dropped to 16.6%, the most precipitous drop to occur during any presidential administration. Like Roosevelt, Reagan knew that unions provided the only real leverage for workers in a capitalist economy. Unlike Roosevelt, Reagan had no interest in protecting that leverage. Rather, his intention was to take it away. His administration had no interest in providing a livable wage to the bottom tier of working American citizens, so the federal minimum wage stayed frozen at $3.35 per hour throughout Reagan's eight years.

To take the nation's elderly out of poverty, Roosevelt established the Social Security Administration.

Reagan taxed Social Security benefits for the first time. He also took money out of the Social Security Trust Fund for the first time. A 2013 article by Allen W. Smith gives the details on how Reagan passed an increase in the payroll tax {which funds the Social Security Trust Fund} to "secure the future of Social Security." However, instead of the payroll tax hike {which generated $2.7 trillion over three decades} going into the Social Security Trust Fund to make the fund solvent into the future, it went into the general fund to reduce the debt created by Reagan's tax cuts for the wealthy.

The tax on social security, coupled with the increased payroll tax, did reduce the debt created by Reagan's tax cut for the wealthy, but even this one-two-punch could not cover it all. The Reagan years saw the national debt more than double. The pirating of the revenue generated by the increased payroll tax resulted in thirty years of 'borrowing' from the Social Security trust fund money that will, in all probability, never be paid back. Remember that the Payroll tax to fund the Social Security system stops being collected once a taxpayer's income reaches a certain level. Thus, the wealthy pay very little of the tax as a percentage of their income, making this entire scheme a $2.7 trillion tax hike on the middle class to pay for a tax break for the wealthy. Given this history, would it not seem appropriate now for Congress to levy a 'wealth tax' on the wealthy class that has seen the benefits of the tax cuts borrowed Social Security money paid for, in order to pay back the $2.7 trillion?

The second, more sinister objective of keeping the increased funds out of the Social Security trust fund was to keep the fund from becoming "solvent well into the future." Republicans, including Reagan, have never liked the Social Security system. At the time the increase in the payroll tax passed, Senator Daniel Patrick Moynihan, noting that the money was not going into the Social Security trust fund, called it thievery. Today as elected officials discuss cutting social security benefits, or raising contribution levels to make the system 'solvent into the future', what you don't hear discussed is the repayment of the money stolen from the fund. Neither party, Republican or Democrat, will bring up the subject in hopes that the American people will not focus on the thievery.

To curb greedy abuse by wealthy financial operators, Roosevelt established the Security and Exchange Commission to regulate their activities. He enacted the Glass Steagall Act to provide safer, less speculative use of financial institution's assets. He created the Federal Deposit Insurance Corporation to protect individual deposits and give consumers faith in the banking industry. His policies resulted in fifty years of relative stability in the financial industry.

Reagan loosened regulations beginning with The Garn-St.Germain Depository Institutions Act in 1982 deregulated the savings and loan industry. This action was instrumental in bringing on the savings and loan scandal of 1991, in which hundreds of savings and loan institutions collapsed while the Federal Savings and Loan Insurance Corporation became insolvent. This all resulted in a $132 billion bailout at taxpayer's expense as they were forced to pay for the de-regulation.

The Security and Exchange Commission under Reagan adopted Rule 10B-18 (The Safe Harbor provision), making stock buy-backs legal for the first time, thereby providing a tool for future abuse by financiers to manipulate stock prices. The party that formerly claimed to stand for fiscal responsibility had no problem with Reagan's deficit spending or with providing bail-out money when his de-regulation policies backfired.

Roosevelt's policies created a strong, vibrant middle class, while Reagan's policies helped to destroy it. An April 2022 study by the PEW Institute concluded that middle-income households in America had shrunk from 61% in 1980 to 50% in 2022. Unfortunately, the destruction continued beyond the Reagan Administration. With the selection of William Clinton as their party standard bearer, the Democrats took their own turn to the right and away from the Roosevelt policies.

The Clinton Administration did little to reverse the ever growing wealth and income gap. What Clinton did do was repeal the Glass Steagall Act, contributing to the financial collapse and Great Recession of 2006. The 2006 financial crises resulted in a $700 billion federal bailout of the financial sector. Once again, the American taxpayer picked up the tab for de-regulation. After fifty years of relative stability, Reagan and Clinton's easing of regulations on the financial industry caused instability in financial sectors, costing taxpayers billions. Never learning from our mistakes, the American people just elected a new president who promises to 'cut regulations'. It would be prudent to keep the results of past de-regulation efforts in mind as the Trump administration enacts their agenda.

Subsequent tax reduction acts in the George W. Bush and the Trump administration gave the great majority of tax relief benefits to the wealthiest individual. Their tax changes also cut corporate taxpayers widening the wealth gap while swelling the national debt. The percentage of total tax collections coming from corporate America and the wealthiest citizens continued to shrink.

In a June 2011 article written for the Economic Policy Institute, Andrew Fieldhouse wrote, the "Bush Tax cuts remain expensive, ineffective and unfair." The Texas A & M professor goes on to say they "conferred disproportionate benefits to those at the top of the earnings distribution, exacerbating a trend of widening income inequality at a time of already poor wage growth. The one % of earners received 38% of the Bush tax cuts, the lower 60% less than 20%."

An analysis in July 2012 done by Chye-Ching and Nathaniel Frentz for the Center on Budget and Policy Priorities came to similar conclusions. They wrote, 'The Bush tax cuts in 2001 and 2003 made the tax code less progressive and delivered a large windfall to the highest income taxpayers. The cuts increased after-tax income for the highest-income taxpayers by more than 7.3% but increased after-tax income for the bottom 20% by just 2.8%. Despite all this information, on January 1, 2013, when these tax cuts were due to expire, they could only be extended with the consent of the president. President Obama signed a bill extending most of the original provisions of the cuts, giving Congressional Republicans a huge victory and the Obama administration a part in the growth of the widening wealth gap.

The Trump tax cuts performed even worse for middle-class taxpayers. In their book, 'The Triumph of Injustice,' University of California at Berkeley economists Emmanuel Saeza and Gabriel Zucman calculate that the results of this tax bill are that 'the top 400 richest families in the United States paid an average effective tax rate of 23% while the bottom half of American households paid a rate of 24.2%'. For the first time in America's history, billionaires pay taxes at a lower rate than the middle class.

Thus, the main ingredient in creating an oligarchy, the concentration of wealth has been put in place. A PEW institute study concluded that the wealth gap in America today is at its greatest level since 1928, as the bottom 90% of the country shares less than 50% of all pretax income for the first time since statistics have been kept. Much of the cause of this shift is the income tax changes over the past forty years. The Republican Party continues to cater to the wealthiest among us while holding to the Ayn Rand philosophy that selfishness is better than the concept of a common good. The Democrats, as noted, have also contributed, and their biggest contribution has been their lack of an action to correct the situation when they had the numbers to do so. The wealth gap that has been created is often cited as one of the chief threats to democracy. As we witness Elon Musk exercise the power within the transition team it becomes clear that the 2024 election has resulted in the complete takeover of the wheels of government by the billionaire class. As I write this chapter Elon Musk, a private citizen who holds no position in government, a billionaire with a number of very lucrative contracts with the U.S. government, is orchestrating a government shutdown over the 2024 Christmas season. He is blatantly taking control of the House Republican Caucus dictating the direction they should take leading up to the day Trump takes office. So far the House Speaker has shown little willingness, or ability to exercise control over Musk's wishes. In addition to the obvious conflict of interest involved in a billionaire industrialist who contracts with the government directing policy in the Congress, this constitutes a clear example of the control of the wheels of government by the elite billionaire class we have created. Is this what the American people want? Is this what they voted for in November? Trump has promised even more tax cuts for the wealthy as well as another corporate tax cut which will only make matters worse. With this administration over the next four years we can expect the wealth and income gap to reach new levels.

In his book 'Perfectly Legal,' David Cay Johnston called the tax changes "the covert campaign to rig our tax system to benefit the super-rich and cheat everybody else." He cites studies by organizations like the Center for Budget and Policy Priorities, the Congressional Budget Office, and the National Bureau of Economic Research that all support the PEW

Institute's finding that the wealth and income gap in America is on a level not seen since the Gilded Age.

Another study by Thomas Piketty and Emanuel Saez concluded that over three decades, the share of national income by the bottom 90% fell from 2/3 to slightly more than half, while the top 10% of the nation's share went from 33% to 40%. Furthermore, within the top 10%, the highest-income earners reap the greatest benefits. A May 2023 report by the Brookings Institute concluded that wealth inequality in America is today as close to the peak levels in the Gilded Age as we have ever been.

Despite the claims, there is little or no evidence that any of these tax cuts inspired economic or job growth. The end results of the Reagan, Bush, and Trump tax cuts have been that the top 400 richest families in America who paid taxes at a rate of 40% in 1980 now pay at a rate of 23% (again from the same book). This is as the country continues to run huge deficits, and the wealth and income gap continues to widen. The channeling of money meant for the Social Security System coupled with these tax cuts has been a hard-hitting one/two punch for average, working class Americans all for the benefit of the wealthy. Despite all this, working class Americans continue to elect the same culprits, espousing the same trickle down bologna to office. The most recent election ushered more self-serving, wealthy individuals into seats of power in the Senate as well as the administration.

Today, the top 1% of the nation's income earners control fifteen times more wealth than the bottom 50% combined, according to Professor Robert Reich. A study by the Institute for Economic Equity in July of 2023 offered that the top 10% of households as a group held 69% of wealth while the bottom 50% held 2.4%. Where is the outrage from the bottom 90% of Americans who have been robbed by this tremendous transfer of wealth?

In addition to the obscene tax cuts for the wealthy, growth in income figures for the wealthy are staggering. A report authored by The Economic Policy Institute in October of 2022 cited the amazing growth of pay at the upper level of positions in corporate America compared to the very modest growth among workers. According to the report, CEO to typical worker pay in 1965 was 20 to 1, while in 2021, it had grown to 399 to 1. This is a wider gap than is present in any other developed country in the world. The report goes on to say that from 1978 to 2021, worker productivity has increased by 64.8% while worker pay has only increased by 17.3%, but CEO pay has increased by 1.460.2%. This disparity has helped fuel the growth of the income and wealth of the top 1%, and contributes to the rising inequality. Again this disparity has caused no outrage from the 90% at the bottom. Voters continue to elect politicians that support the very policies that have created the current inequality.

What has not been measured is the level of lost hope among the 90% of the public that has been left behind. As middle and lower-class American workers lay awake at night worried because they have inadequate or nonexistent health insurance, worried about a lack of resources to educate their children, or worried about countless other problems, any hope of getting ahead is lost. How much has the loss of hope for their future caused an increase in crime and/or drug use? This is a subject which would make for an interesting sociological study.

We live at a time when American military veterans are homeless, living in the streets, while billionaires build rockets to launch themselves into space. Something has gone wrong in our country, and the outrage that should be rampant at this disparity is virtually nonexistent. On November fifth the country elected a member of the billionaire class to the office of president. Do those who voted for Trump truly believe he will change any of the financial abuse they have collectively suffered? Is the voting public that naïve?

The two initiatives in the creation of this Oligarchy were the relentless efforts to restrict voting rights and the creation of an elite class. So now, the elite class has been created over the past forty years, and the necessary pieces have been put in place.

The final piece of the puzzle necessary to build an oligarchy is to create a system in which the concentrated wealth can be put to use to provide control. The means by which this special class of Americans can control the system has also been put in place with the assistance of the Roberts-led Supreme Court and the actions of Congress. The efforts to limit the ability to vote and to have your vote count, coupled with the final ingredient, money in politics, have provided the means for control by the wealthy class. Their control is accomplished through their bankrolling of campaigns, plus their money spent on lobbying. Their control is evidenced by the policy actions of Congress which attest to the success of the investments by the wealthy class.

> *"We can have democracy in this country, or we can have great wealth concentrated in the hands of a few, but we can't have both."*
>
> *Former Supreme Court Justice,*
> *Louis Dembitz Brandeis*

CHAPTER 6

MONEY IN POLITICS

"We must especially beware of that small group of selfish men who would clip the Wings of the American Eagle in order to feather their own nest."

FDR

Mitt Romney was working a rope line at the Iowa State Fair when he was running for President of the United States in 2011. A few activists very loudly challenged him on his pledge to not raise taxes, urging him to raise taxes on the wealthy. He did not back down, emphasizing that, in his opinion, raising taxes hurts people. Then, a fellow shouted

DEMOCRACY

out a one-word challenge: "Corporations." Romney looked up and smiled. "Corporations are people, my friend," he said, giving a line that became famous.

Presidential candidate Hillary Clinton was the subject of a serious bashing in a paid "documentary" funded entirely by corporate political action committees in opposition to her campaign. After the main group behind the paid political hit piece was denied airtime by the Federal Elections Commission under the auspices of the Bipartisan Campaign Reform Act, they went to Court. The subsequent decision by the Supreme Court in their case, Citizens United v. United States Federal Election Commission, established that monetary expenditures are a protected form of free speech.

Corporations are people, a metamorphosis from a developed entity to operate as a cohesive, single enterprise on behalf of owners and investors, to a person. Money is speech, a transformation of money from a medium of exchange to a protected form of political expression. This is the backdrop of how we view campaign financing today. Money is not free speech, it is currency meant to be used for making a purchase. When a person or corporation heaps lavish gifts on a Supreme Court Justice, or gives large amounts of money to a candidate's campaign they have indeed made a purchase. This fact is the crux of the problem with money in politics. Unfortunately, today the American people have come to accept, and feel its normal for the wealthiest corporations and individuals to spend hundreds of millions of dollars to influence election results. In effect it has become an acceptable practice to buy elections and the most recent election is a prime example. How have the American people been convinced that it is acceptable for one individual to throw more than $250 million into a presidential campaign? Are we naïve enough to believe that a contribution that large will not result in an even larger return on the 'investment.'

The increasing influence of money in political campaigning has been a source of concern for some in our nation for a number of years, yet efforts to address the problem have failed miserably. The obscene amounts of money spent on campaigns have grown to staggering levels. While we view with disgust the examples of individuals within the system being corrupt, we have sat quietly as the entire system has become corrupt right before our eyes. In the 2020 election, over $14 billion was spent on races for the Presidency, Senate, and the U.S. House, according to the Center for Responsive Politics. The final totals are not yet in for the 2024 campaigns, but Open Secrets estimates that we will break the 2020 record by spending $16 billion plus in total. Just eight years ago in the 2016 presidential election year the total spending equaled $6.5 billion. Even more disturbing, the percentage of money raised by 'small donors' {under $200} for these cycles has been less than 20% as wealthy interests dominate fund raising.

In my home state of Maine, a state with less than 1.4 million residents, the 2020 Senate race between Senator Susan Collins and her opponent Sara Gideon produced nearly $100 million in donations to the two sides. Every election year the influence of money in the electoral process grows. Nine of the ten most expensive Senate races of all time happened in 2020, and the nine races cost a combined $2.1 billion. The Senate race in North Carolina led the way, registering a total cost of $298.9 million, followed closely by the South Carolina Senate race, which cost $276.9 million. These records may be broken with the final tallies are in for 2024.

There are federal limits on the amount of money that can be contributed to a campaign;

- An individual is limited to $3,300 in any election cycle, meaning that amount in the primary and the same amount in the general election.

- A campaign committee can give $2,000 per election cycle.

- A multi-candidate PAC can give $5,000 per cycle.

- A non-multi candidate PAC can give $2,000 per cycle.

- A State/district/local party committee can give $5,000 per cycle.

- A national party committee can give $5,000 per cycle.

With these limits on the amount of money that can be contributed to a candidate, how can millions of dollars coming from one source be involved in campaigns? With those limits in place, how is it possible that wealthy individuals and corporations can throw millions of dollars into one candidate's campaign?

The answer lies in the rulings by our Supreme Court that have made it impossible to control the amount of money that can be raised and spent on political campaigns. The Courts ruling in Citizens United brought about the advent of 'Super PAC's'. These new PAC's are independent expenditure only political committees that may accept, and expend unlimited contributions from individuals, corporations, and Unions. In theory these PAC's while spending money to support a candidate are operating independently of the candidates campaign with absolutely no interaction or coordination. The idea that there is no contact between the campaign and the efforts of the Super PAC is pure fantasy.

The idea that all this money has no effect on the policies that flow from Washington {or from state capitols for that matter} is beyond naive. With such a flood of money in our electoral process, is it any wonder that this corrupt system would produce a candidate for President who has dedicated his entire life to a greedy pursuit of wealth gained by any means, legal or illegal?

Just as in the case of voting rights, the Supreme Court has played a major role in the polluting of our electoral system with money. When reviewing the Supreme Court's decisions on voting restrictions and money in politics, it is important to look at how Supreme Court Justices gain their seats on the Court. The Federalist Society was formed in 1982 and headed by a man named Leonard Leo, who continues as its head today. Leo's organization and its influence has grown over the past forty years to extraordinary levels, and now his 'society' enjoys great control over appointments to the bench. Leo has built a network of related agencies under the umbrella of the Federalist Society, like the Marble Freedom Trust and the Judicial Confirmation Network, all of which raise billions of dollars to influence Congress as well as public opinion. His network is yet another example of how money controls America. The appointment of easily influenced, conservative Supreme Court Justices starts with Leo's influence, and their rulings affect the everyday lives of every American. Since the founding of the Federalist Society, Antonin Scalia, Clarence Thomas, John Roberts, Samuel Alito, Neil Gorsuch, and Brett Kavanaugh, all card-carrying members of the Federalist Society have been appointed to the Court.

Their nominations were all backed by confirmation campaigns funded by Leo's organization. These conservative justices have given us the Citizens United decision and the rulings that stripped out the key sections of the Voting Rights Act amongst others. Their appointments to the Court were intended to lend judicial support to the attacks on voting rights and the corruption of our electoral process with money, and they have performed admirably. The decisions of the Supreme Court over the past three decades have had as much to do with the decline of American Democracy as the actions of elected officials. It can be argued that Chief Justice Roberts has done more to subvert our Democracy than any other American.

Not satisfied with his destructive influence on the nation's courts, Leo has now begun spreading his dark money to other initiatives. In the election of 2024 Leo announced his intention to spend huge amounts of 'dark money' on State Legislative races. In my home state of Maine he threw $375,000 into legislative races {according to a report in the Bangor Daily News} to help elect MAGA candidates. The fact that a little known, unelected man of such limited skills can exercise so much influence on the issues that shape our nation is a disgusting example of how money has so corrupted our system. Without the stream of funding from billionaires for Leo's various organizations it's doubtful anyone would have ever heard of Leonard Leo.

What is yet another bastardization of our Democracy is that the current majority of the Court has been appointed by presidents who lost the popular vote. John Roberts and Samuel Alito were appointed by George W Bush, and Neil Gorsuch, Brett Kavanaugh, and Amy Coney Barrett by Trump. In addition, the nominations were confirmed by Senators representing a minority of the population because of the makeup of the Senate. One hundred and eleven million people live in the states of California, New York, Texas, and Florida, roughly a third of the three hundred and thirty-two million people in America. A little less than three million people live in the states of North and South Dakota, Wyoming, and Vermont, yet the two sets of four states have the same eight members of the Senate that confirm judicial appointments. It used to take a two-thirds vote of the Senate to confirm judicial appointments, which would have made confirmation by Senators representing less than half the population more difficult. That was changed by the Democrats in 2013 for lower-level appointments and later changed by the Republicans to include Supreme Court appointments. With the current requirement of a simple majority vote, Justices can be confirmed by a vote in the Senate that may not represent a majority of the people. Removing the sixty percent requirement has made judicial appointments a purely partisan exercise resulting in a Supreme Court made up of purely politically partisan Justices.

On January 21, 2010, the United States Supreme Court issued its disastrous ruling in Citizen's United v Federal Election Commission, a decision that created a new era in campaign spending. By a 5-4 vote, the Roberts Court ruled that the Freedom of Speech clause of the First Amendment prohibits the government from restricting independent expenditures for political campaigns by corporations, including nonprofit corporations, labor unions, and other organizations. With his attacks on voting rights coupled with his rulings on money in our political system, it's easy to see Chief Justice John Roberts as a leader in the attacks on our Democracy. As mentioned earlier, the decision gave birth to new forms of Political Action Committees (PACs), like separated funds (SSFs), non-connected committees and Super PACs which are all allowed to solicit and distribute funds. No other democratic country allows its political process to be so polluted by money. The money flowing into these PACs is extremely difficult to trace back to its origins, thus the term 'Dark Money.' Once the wealth of the nation has been concentrated in the hands of the few, the next step is to create a political system completely corrupted and controlled by money. This is so that those with great wealth can manipulate the system to perpetuate their ability to maintain and grow their wealth. A series of Supreme Court rulings culminating in the Citizens United case by the Roberts Court has created just such a system. In a 2011 CNN, Gallup poll, 67% of respondents agreed that political races in America were decided strictly by money. In the thirteen years since that poll things have gotten so much worse as the amount of money influencing our elections has skyrocketed.

These new PAC's using 'dark money,' the source of which is not identifiable, has enabled the wealthiest corporations and individuals to spend unlimited amounts of money to support the candidates of their choice, and to thereby influence decision-making. The increase in money spent on lobbyists since the Citizens United ruling is indicative of the efforts to influence decision-making at the Congressional level. In the book "Perfectly Legal" David Cay Johnson writes that highly paid tax consultants provide to the super wealthy ways in which they can avoid paying taxes. The consultants are well versed in the loopholes they advise their clientele on because they write the loopholes and then lobby Congress to get them into the tax code.

The new PACS created after the Citizens ruling are allowed to spend unlimited amounts from unrestricted sources so long as the spending is independent of the candidate's campaign or political

DEMOCRACY

party. The creation of these PAC rules has made it impossible to control fundraising. A wealthy person or corporation can place millions of dollars in the PAC and use it to promote the same candidate, thereby making finance restrictions meaningless. As one example, George Soros funded his PAC with $175 million in support of Democrats.

In the Presidential campaign of 2024 both candidates, Trump and Harris, received millions from wealthy donors. Both of their campaigns were funded as much as a third to a half by billionaires and large corporations. The list of the largest contributors to each campaign reads like a who's who of American billionaires. Some of the major players involved;

- Microsoft founder Bill Gates reportedly contributed up to $50 million to the Harris camp.

- Elon Musk campaigned with, and contributed over $250 million to Trump.

- Former New York Mayor Michael Bloomberg reportedly contributed nearly $50 million to the Harris campaign.

- Miriam Adelson, widow of Sheldon Adelson contributed a reported $90 million to the Trump election effort.

The list goes on for Trump, Blackstone CEO Steve Schwarzman, Texas Banker Andrew Beal, and Diane Hendricks, and for Harris, Reed Hastings, Reid Hoffman and Michelle Yee, Sam Altman, and David Ellison to name just a few. Money from billionaires also flowed freely into PAC's supporting efforts by both Parties to gain control of both houses of the Congress. Take the case of Citadel Securities founder, Ken Griffin. He is responsible for more than $100 million in donations, $30 million to the Republican Senate Leadership fund, and $17 million to the Congressional Leadership fund. In most cases these donations to House and Senate campaigns were in addition to presidential campaign donations. The final campaign figures for 2024 were not available at the time of this writing but clearly money from the wealthiest individuals and corporations in the country played a major if not the major role in the outcome.

So what does all this money buy for the contributors? In the most basic sense it buys access for their paid lobbyists to influence decision making in Washington. On a more direct example of conflict of interest, Elon Musk has parlayed his contributions to Trump into a major role in the administration. Trump has announced the appointment of Musk to the new position charged with government cost cutting. The various business interests of Musk are closely tied to federal spending. In 2023 Musk's companies signed $3 billion in contracts with seventeen federal agencies. SpaceX, a Musk company, has close ties with the Pentagon and NASA making it difficult to imagine that his 'cost cutting' efforts will result in any reductions in defense spending. It's Difficult to imagine a more clear cut example of a conflict of interest, but in today's political world, so full of corruption its simply business as usual.

The money does not only flow into campaign coffers and lobbyist pockets; it helps to fund so-called 'think tanks' that work to shape policy. The Koch brothers have provided funding to the Cato Institute and the

Heritage Foundation, two organizations that have a great deal of influence on the Republican agenda. These PACs provide a perfectly legal method for the super-wealthy to finance and control elections, and then to control policy. It is a small wonder that candidates today are afraid of alienating the financiers.

The candidate being promoted by a super PAC is supposed to have no knowledge of the activities of the PAC spending millions on their behalf, but this is almost never the case. It is difficult to prove collaboration between the two but extremely naïve to conclude it is not there. This heavy spending by special PACs has resulted in sapping the influence of average Americans.

The result of all this is that Congressional and presidential races are financed to an ever increasing extent by the top 1 percent of the wealthiest Americans and the wealthiest corporations in the country. These same financiers of the campaigns then spend exorbitant amounts of money on lobbying efforts. It is a very safe assumption that the money spent by the wealthy on campaigns and lobbyists is not being used to influence policymakers for the benefit of the working class.

The combination of concentrated wealth and the current political system with so much money involved provides the means by which a small, well-healed group can rule the country by means of an electoral system corrupted by money. This is the very definition of an oligarchy, as well as a perfect formula to perpetuate the wealth disparity that created the Oligarchy in the first place.

> *"There is no enemy of free government more dangerous and none so insidious as the corruption of the electoral process"*
>
> ***President Teddy Roosevelt***

It has been a well-planned and well-carried-out effort by the Republican Party since 1980. The system was created, and then supported by conservative judges like Chief Justice Roberts who have been appointed to ensure that the courts support the money sources and voter suppression. For their part, the Democrats have stood by numbly watching it happen, placated in their silence by the same money that has bastardized the system. One wonders what FDR, Truman, and Kennedy would think of today's lackluster Democratic Party.

LOBBYING EXPENDITURES

Coupled with the money spent on political campaigns is the excessive amount of money now spent on lobbying efforts. Campaign contributions are made to elect the candidates the moneyed interests want, money spent on lobbyists is intended to ensure that the chosen candidates vote the right way. If the chosen candidates do not support the policy positions important to their benefactors, the flow of money will be turned off. What's more, the office holder that does not follow directions may well end up with a heavily financed primary opponent. This threat of a primary is very effective given that the primary focus of the majority of today's office holders is to hold on to the power of their office.

According to Open Secret's analysis of lobbying expenditures, $4.1 billion was spent in 2022 to influence the votes in Congress. In the first three months of 2023, organizations employed 10,550 federal lobbyists at a cost of over $1 billion over the three months setting a pace to match the 2022 spending.

In an article by Lee Drutman published in the Atlantic, he points out that "for every dollar spent on lobbying by labor unions and public interest groups together, large corporations and their associates spend $34." He goes on to observe that "one has to go back to the Gilded Age to find business in such a dominant political position in America."

So, Citizens United defines corporations as citizens while also defining money as free speech. The result is skyrocketing money from the wealthiest in the nation channeled into campaigns and lobbying efforts to influence decisions. Concentration of wealth, and voter restrictions are the first two ingredients to creating an oligarchy. Those at the top who benefit the most from that concentration will influence the policy making process to see to it that wealth stays concentrated in that small group, the very definition of an oligarchy.

How could Democracy in the United States, as the cherished form of government for two hundred years, be in such peril? How could it decline into this state in a nation where thousands have given their lives to sustain it as their form of government? The answer lies in a collective effort over forty years by people more concerned with gaining wealth and maintaining power than in governing a nation and maintaining a democracy. As Lincoln put it, "As a nation of free men, we must live through all time or die by suicide", the tools of suicide in America today are greed and power.

DEMOCRACY

MEANS OF CONTROL

"American fascists claim to be super-patriots, but they would destroy every Liberty that is guaranteed by the Constitution. They demand free enterprise but are the spokesmen for monopoly and vested interest. Their final objective is to capture political power so that, using the power of the state and the power of the market simultaneously, they may keep the common man in eternal subjection."

Vice President Henry Wallace

The statement by the Vice President was made in 1944 in reference to the fascist movement in Europe that had gained some traction in the United States. The reference to using the power of the state in conjunction with the power of the market is as applicable to today's wealthy class as it was to a different group in 1944. The wealthy elite class necessary for an oligarchy to function has been created over the forty-year period from 1980 to 2020. The structure necessary for that elite group to exercise control has largely been established over the same period. It has one tool available to exercise control, and that tool is money, money, and more money. Once the great wealth transfer has been accomplished, it must be made easy for the top 10% to use that wealth to control the process.

The Reagan administration began the process of transferring wealth from the middle class to the top ten percent of the wealthiest Americans. Subsequent Republican administrations, seeing the success of the Reagan formulae, have continued the transfer, even accelerating the pace. The tremendous transfer of wealth happened in the plain view of working-class America, yet many of the people adversely affected by his policies continue to think of Reagan as a great president. The acceptance of this thievery by the public is so complete that after passing his tax cut that benefitted the richest Americans, Trump felt comfortable announcing to a gathering of billionaires that "I just made you even richer." To this announcement, the group gathered in an exclusive private club most Americans would not be allowed to enter gave enthusiastic applause. Even as the continued wealth transfer is rubbed in their face, voters chose to elect Trump to a second term.

"It's a private club, and you ain't in it."
George Carlin

CHAPTER 7

CORRUPTION

"We have created new idols. The worship of the ancient golden calf has returned in a new and ruthless guise in the idolatry of money and the dictatorship of an impersonal economy lacking a truly human purpose."

His Holiness, Pope Francis

To be sure, corruption in the political process is as old as the government itself. It has existed in America for years, with some prime examples being the Teapot Scandal during the Harding administration, the Whiskey Ring, and Star Route scandals during the U. S. Grant Presidency, and of course, the Watergate scandal and the Iran Contra affair. In periods of increased prosperity, such as the Gilded Age, corruption seems to peak. This is especially true when that prosperity is concentrated in a particularly small group at the top. This was the case in the Gilded Age, and it is the case today. The question today is; has corruption hit new heights in America? Moreover, have things that happen every day, in plain sight, become accepted when, at another time, they would have been considered scandalous? We have had scandals in the past that involved the corruption of an official or group of officials, and while this still happens, today we are also looking at the corruption of the entire system. A system corrupted by practices that have become accepted over time that involve millions of dollars. The scandalous amounts of money that today channel through our political system by means that have become legal would have been considered corrupt in the past.

During the first Trump administration a half dozen members of his cabinet resigned in some cases under the cloud of scandal. Criminal charges were recommended in several cases with the Trump Justice Department choosing not to pursue the charges. The list of members of Trump's inner circle of advisors that have been convicted of a crime is exceptionally long;

> Steve Bannon—Contempt of Congress
> Michael Flynn—Lying to the FBI
> George Papadopoulos—Lying to the FBI
> Peter Navarro—Contempt of Congress
> Michael Cohen—Campaign Finance Charges
> Paul Manafort—Tax and Bank Fraud
> Roger Stone—Obstruction of Justice, Witness Tampering, Lying to Congress
> Rick Gates—Lying to Congress
> Allen Weissenberg--Perjury

Jared Kushner, President Trump's son-in law, was given a job in the White House in violation of the practice against nepotism. After he left the administration he walked away with a two billion dollar 'investment' by the Saudi Investment Fund into his fledgling firm. These are just some of the individual scandals in the first Trump administration. Coupled with his own criminal activity these individual cases are enough to brand his first term the most scandalous, corrupt administration in our history. In spite of it all voters chose to elect him again anyway. His re-election stands as the proof of the reality that our country has come to accept corruption at the highest levels of our government.

The corruption of our entire system is even more disturbing than the record of the first Trump administration. Today, nearly every office holder in Congress gives open access to lobbyists who are being paid by the very same benefactors that finance the campaigns of these senators and house members. This happens routinely as these paid lobbyists present the interests of their employers on key pieces of legislation. The main reason they gain the ear of a particular member of Congress is the money provided to that elected official when they campaigned. The effect of this paid access is aptly demonstrated by the actions, and inactions of our leaders. This can be demonstrated in the cases of the fossil fuel industry and the pharmaceutical industry. While these two industries are prime examples, they are only two among many.

As climate change, the environmental crisis of our time has steadily worsened Congress has strongly resisted taking any meaningful action to curtail the use of fossil fuels. The overwhelming majority of scientists agree that the use of fossil fuels is a prime cause of climate change, yet Congress has literally fiddled while the world is burning. Much of the United States and Canada have experienced terrible out-of-control wildfires that have sent plumes of dangerous smoke across both nations. Still other areas have suffered through flooding. All this has happened in recent years yet the oil and coal lobby works hard to keep Congress from acting, and one needs to look no further than the contributions of the industry players to understand the inaction. The major companies like Exon Mobil and British

Petroleum fund their own lobbying while still contributing to the American Petroleum Institute which employs hundreds of lobbyists. The lobbying efforts are not confined to Congress, as efforts are routinely made to sabotage climate conferences around the world as well as to finance publicity campaigns to win public support.

Coupled with the lobby expenditures are very generous campaign contributions. Statista Research Department reports that the fossil fuel industry contributed $63.6 million to campaigns in 2020 with more than two thirds going to Republicans. In the months leading up to the 2024 election presidential candidate Trump publicly offered the fuel industry favorable tax and environmental regulations during his administration in exchange for a billion dollar campaign contribution. While the industry stopped short of a billion dollars Trump received record donations form the oil industry. At nearly $15 million the industry was Trump's fourth largest source of corporate funding.

Oil Change International reported that in 2013/2014 total campaign and lobbying expenditures by the industry of more than $350 million. The same report shows that all this money has paid off in more than the inaction on climate change. While opponents of renewable energy bemoan the subsidies for wind and solar, fossil fuels do quite well in that regard. In the same two-year period, 2013/2014, the Federal Government paid out $41.8 billion in exploration and production subsidies. Certainly, seems the money spent is paying off quite handsomely. As for the coal industry, we continue to produce and burn coal even though the carbon emissions cannot be dealt with in any environmentally friendly manner. Elected officials ignore the environmental harm in order to gain the contributions giving them ample funding to maintain their seat of power.

Adding to all this, there is a long list of executives from the fossil fuel industry landing key positions in presidential administrations over the years. Most recently, the Trump team included Exon Mobile CEO Rex Tillerson as his first Secretary of State. George

W. Bush and his father were both former industry senior executives before becoming President. The same is true of former Vice President Dick Chaney. In his American Prospect article for Open Secrets Alex Kotch wrote that members of Congress own over $93 million in fossil fuel stock, so the heavy investment in the industry by office holders may be yet another factor to explain the inaction. If the fossil fuel monies continue to flow into campaign coffers, the resistance to action against climate change will continue. With the results of the election on November 5th we can expect continued favorable treatment of the fossil fuel industry for the coming years. Trump has openly aired his objections to nearly every environmental agreement entered into by previous administrations that were intended to address climate change. He refers to climate change as "a hoax". He continues to voice his opposition to alternative 'clean energy' sources, and can be expected to oppose their development.

In the case of the pharmaceutical industry, the very reasonable proposal to allow the Medicare health insurance program to negotiate prescription drug prices has always been met with resistance in Congress. The resistance has remained constant even as American consumers pay more for the same medications than people in other countries. The Congressional opposition can be traced to the $373 million spent on lobbying by the pharmaceutical and health products industry, as reported by Statista Research.

President Biden took unilateral action, bypassing Congress, and as of September 2023, the Medicare health insurance program can begin negotiating for some prescription drug prices. Predictably, the President's actions were challenged in Court, and the program was upheld by a federal judge. Again we can expect our new administration to halt any progress in this area.

In perhaps the worst case of the inability of Congress to take action in an ongoing problem is the case of gun violence and the influence of the National Rifle Association. On October 25, 2023, eighteen people were shot to death in quiet, peaceful Lewiston, Maine. They were shot to death by a man with an assault weapon he should not have owned. The shooter involved had a recent history of mental illness that was ignored to the point that he was able to legally purchase an assault weapon. The event was one of 565 mass shootings in the United States in 2023. The problem of gun violence in America is far more prevalent than in any other country on the planet, yet with mass shootings occurring year after year very little is done by the Congress to address the problem. Our elected officials are so afraid of crossing the gun lobby that the safety of the citizens takes a back seat to the importance of them holding on to the support of the gun lobby to maintain the power of their office. Our elected leaders would rather witness more school shootings than risk losing their seats in congress.

There has long been a very cozy relationship between defense contractors and the Pentagon. The new Trump administration will be bringing that cozy relationship to a new level through Trump's own cozy relationship with Elon Musk, but more about that later. It's been over sixty years since outgoing President Eisenhower warned us of the "military industrial complex" which is even a more robust relationship today than it was then. The U.S. defense budget is larger than the next ten countries combined, but the defense contractors have been successful in making defense spending untouchable. Efforts by Congress and by past administrations to reduce spending usually begin with an agreement that defense spending is off the table. In the 2020 elections defense contractors contributed over $51 million to various friendly candidates in both political parties according to Open Secrets. The leading contributors included Lockheed Martin, Raytheon Technologies, and Northrop Grumman, with all three throwing in over $5 million. Defense contractors repeated the performance in 2024 contributing over $50 million to various friendly candidates.

All this spending, with the related favorable results in Congress and with the executive branch, begs the question: Are these practices which are now acceptable, nonetheless corrupt? These transactions happen on a daily basis and involve the great majority of office holders. What's more, the public is aware of the practice, and we express no outrage that our elected officials seem to be bought and paid for as reflected by their actions. Not only do we not show any outrage, we return these same players to their elected positions every two years with the assistance of their huge campaign budgets. The longer they hold office, the more blatant becomes the money that flows their way. The figures quoted here only include the reported campaign contributions and lobbying expenditures. What's not included are the perks, the gifts, the free dinners, and Washington D.C. parties thrown by the same industries in order to wine and dine decision makers.

The answer to the question is yes, this is all corrupt. It's now accepted, it's done in plain sight and the great majority of office holders are greedy participants, but it is corrupt. As long as political campaigns in America require vast amounts of money, and as long as the PAC regulations remain in place, these practices will continue because our elected representatives are forced to spend more time raising money than they do analyzing the issues before them. The entire system is so polluted with cash that it's outrageously corrupt right in plain sight. All this corrupt spending is the reality of the state of our government, a government functioning as an Oligarchy not as a Democracy.

Congressional members and other government officials being charged with insider trading happens all too frequently as the stock trading while serving in public office goes on daily with only the most blatant cases being brought to the justice department. These are all examples of what can be referred to as 'system corruption' in that they are not necessarily caused by officials lacking the ability to act within ethical standards {which also happens far too often}. These are common practices that happen with great regularity and have been ongoing now for many years, ongoing for so long that they are now accepted as business as usual. The fact that they have become acceptable does nothing to lessen their impact on the nation's overall morality in its day-to-day operations.

Another example of corruption that happens in plain sight routinely is the practice of family members of elected officials using their relationship to make money. Republicans in the House have investigated actions by President Biden's son, Hunter Biden, in Ukraine and China. The allegation is that he used his father's name to make money while doing business in foreign countries. President Trump's daughter, Ivanka, gained 18 trademarks in China covering her fashion gear so she could do business in that country while her father was serving as President. Her husband, Jarred, as already mentioned, received a two-billion-dollar investment from the Saudis for his private equity firm immediately after serving in the Trump administration. As blatantly wrong as these things are, they do not constitute anything new. Just as in the case of campaign contributions and lobbying expenditures, connections to powerful elected officials have been used for years to open doors for family and friends. The more powerful the office holder the more lucrative the opportunity, Hunter Biden, Jarred Kushner, and Ivanka Trump are simply the latest examples of a long time corrupt practice.

The most disturbing aspect of all these 'business as usual' practices is that they have become accepted as normal. Tax experts advising their rich clients on how to avoid paying taxes are active in Washington working to write the very tax laws involved in the advice they are giving. Major industries using the purchased access to elected officials to stonewall necessary law changes. Family members parlaying their connections into big paydays are all practices related to the greed that has consumed our Democracy and they are all examples of 'system corruption.'

With so much money being poured into our political system, it is a small wonder that corruption would be rampant. So many things have become acceptable now that were not in the past. It is no wonder that corruption seems to happen right before our eyes. Still, we can be shocked by a report that a Supreme Court Justice has received gifts of:

- 38 destination vacations

- 26 private jet flights

- Eight helicopter flights plus voyages on private yachts

- Stays in luxury resorts in Florida and Jamaica

- Golf Club invites, and VIP passes to major sporting events.

- In 33 years on the bench Justice Clarence Thomas has reportedly received 93 gifts worth an estimated $4 million from wealthy benefactors while reporting only 27 on his financial disclosure forms.

These actions of Justice Thomas were described by a former federal Judge, Jeremy Fogel, who served on the Judicial Commission reviewing judges' financial disclosures as "Unprecedented. In my career, I do not remember ever seeing this degree of Largesse given to anybody." Many of these gifts were given by wealthy Americans who had business before the Court. Texas billionaire Harlen Crow purchased Justice Thomas's mother's house plus made tuition payments for one of his relatives. You don't even have to ask if these actions constitute corrupt behavior. The long list of 'favors' bestowed on Justice Thomas dwarfs the $20,000 allegedly gifted to Justice Abe Fortis decades ago that resulted in his resignation. Yet Justice Thomas continues to sit comfortably on the Supreme Court bench. Neither the justice department nor the Congress has made a move to require the Justice to answer for his actions. The fact that Justice Fortis resigned over a $20,000 scandal, while Thomas holds on to his seat after millions of dollars in questionable gifts is indicative of how far we have fallen.

Are we now at a point where even blatant corruption like this will be acceptable? Has rampant corruption now become widespread in the judicial branch? Justice Thomas defends his actions by saying he has not broken any code of conduct basically because the Supreme Court Justices operate without a code of conduct. This is apparently the case as at least three of our current Justices may have committed a felony in order to gain confirmation by the Senate. As pointed out earlier, if President Clinton lied under oath as was claimed, thereby committing a felony, he should have been convicted by the Senate in his impeachment hearing. A case can be made that Justices Gorsuch, Kavanaugh and Coney Barrett all lied to Congress {also a felony}, when asked if the ruling in Roe V. Wade was established precedence not to be overturned. Senator Susan Collins even stated that Kavanaugh lied to her, yet these three justices remain comfortably seated on the Supreme Court Bench after voting to overturn Roe contrary to their Congressional testimony under direct questioning.

Added to the list of questionable actions by Justice Thomas is the involvement of his wife, Virginia Thomas, in the insurrection orchestrated by the Trump team after his loss in the 2020 election. In spite of evidence showing her active participation in the planned coup, Justice Thomas failed to recuse himself when issues involving the matter came before the Court. Most recently, he participated in the decision to entertain the ridiculous claim by Trump's attorneys that he has "absolute immunity" to prosecution by virtue of serving a term as President. This claim had been rejected by the presiding judge in the insurrection case, as well as by a three-judge appellate panel. The unanimous opinion of the Appellate Court was so strong that legal experts were shocked that the Supreme Court would even hear the case but as already covered the High Court not only took it up they ruled in Trump's favor. Justice Thomas was on the 6 to 3 majority opinion. Justice Thomas felt no compulsion to recuse himself in spite of the obvious conflict of interest. To date, Justice Thomas has faced no consequences for his actions. Perhaps this is because a Congress with plenty of dirty laundry of its own is reluctant to point a finger of blame at anyone else.

Recent actions by the courts could lead one to the conclusion that our 'judicial system' is itself intent on obstructing justice in order to protect a former President who appointed many of them. In addition to the high court's ruling on immunity, the Trump-appointed judge in Florida, Aileen Cannon, has issued a series of puzzling decisions in the case alleging Trump stole classified documents. Almost all of Judge Cannon's decisions have been to Trump's advantage right up to her decision to dismiss the case. The dismissal was based on her ruling that the special council who filed the charges was illegally appointed. That ruling was contrary to past decisions involving the same issue, but breaking precedence is no longer an issue when cases involving Trump are concerned.

The so-called 'Emoluments clause" of the Constitution prohibits a sitting president from using the position to increase their wealth. Unlike his predecessors, Donald Trump refused to sever his ties to his financial interests, which could cause a conflict of interest or give an appearance of influencing their policy decisions. Instead of placing his business holdings into a blind trust, there is ample evidence that he, as well as other Trump family members, used his presidency for profit. A study by Open Secrets revealed a pattern of those seeking to curry favor with the President holding various events in Trump hotels and golf resorts. The study provided a long list of political and business groups holding everything from industry conferences to political fundraisers to holiday celebrations in Trump properties and paying exorbitant prices to be there. Even departments within the administration were guilty of holding functions in Trump properties and booking visiting dignitaries into Trump hotels.

U.S. taxpayers have paid Trump properties for security expenses for presidential visits to his own properties as well as security for foreign visitors booked into his hotels. An article by Dan Alexander, senior editor at Forbes, reported that Trump's businesses raked in "2.4 billion of revenue from January 2017 to December 2020," much of which was tied to his position as President. The Trump family claimed to have "put a hold" on foreign dealings during his presidency. However, a report by Rebecca Jacobs and Robert Maguire claims that Trump made $160 million from international business dealings while President. Their article goes on to detail instances in which they make the case that his foreign business holdings influenced his decision-making. He surprisingly pulled U.S. troops out of Syria, reversing a commitment to the Kurds, for the benefit of Turkey, a country in which Trump held several business interests. He lifted the ban that kept Chinese telecommunications company ZTE from doing business in America. The company's inability to acquire parts and software from American companies was pushing it to bankruptcy. At the time he lifted the ban, his daughter was in the process of acquiring Chinese trademarks for her company, while the President held a bank account in China that he had falsely reported had been closed. How much did these monetary entanglements factor into his decision on ZTE? Did his actions at the least present the appearance of a conflict of interest? Of course they did.

Yet with all this evidence of profiteering by President Trump and his family, his campaign to return to the presidency gained support amongst Americans. A second term will surely result in a more robust, well organized effort to gain wealth, but we have come to accept so much corrupt activity as normal that few seem to even care. He is surrounding himself with fellow profiteers, led by Elon Musk, who will use their Trump connection to profit on the backs of U.S. taxpayers.

In violation of the long-standing policy forbidding the President from hiring family, Trump brought his daughter Ivanka, and her husband Jared into his administration. The Republican outrage over President Kennedy's appointment of his brother as Attorney General notwithstanding, he brought them in without objections. He claimed he was not breaking with the policy because the two were working without pay. An analysis by CREW, in an article by Jordon Leibowitz and Caitlin Moniz, estimated that Jared Kushner and Ivanka reported between $172 million and $640 million in outside income while working in the White House. Whatever the true figure in that wide range, the positions the two held in the White House most certainly played a part in their earnings. What's more, as Trump has gained a second term, it is safe to assume that he would re-enter the White House well-versed in how to parlay the office of President into more personal wealth.

Yes, we can be shocked by such reporting, but where is the outrage that Justice Thomas continues to sit on the Court as Congress takes no action? Where was the outrage that the Democrats in the Senate stood behind President Clinton after he allegedly lied under oath? Where is the outrage that only seven Republican Senators voted to impeach President Trump after he inspired an insurrection? Where is the outrage that Democratic Senator Menendez of New Jersey is under indictment for criminal behavior for a second time and refuses to resign? How do we explain the election of a man running for President who had been indicted by four different grand juries in four different parts of the country and was facing 91 felony charges? In addition, he had been convicted of sexually molesting a woman and had been found guilty of fraud on three occasions, plus convicted on 34 felony charges. He and his family have been barred from doing business in New York or being involved in any charitable foundations. Yet, even with that track record, he has been elected for a second term, and his blindly loyal supporters maintain still that he is a victim. Is the country now so comfortable with the corruption and the criminal behavior in our system that we no longer find it objectionable? What kind of example does it set for the youth of America that all this behavior is acceptable?

Apparently, many Americans remain comfortable with a man running the country who is not allowed by law to be connected to a charitable foundation because of his fraudulent behavior. It is a sign of the times we live in that all these offenses are acceptable not only to a majority of the population but also to fellow officials in high-ranking positions. The moral decay of the nation is a contributing factor to the decline of our Democracy. The lack of morality is rampant in our political process so dependent on money. Office holders will do anything necessary to hold on to their position without regard to the corruption in the system that they all participate in feeding. The principles espoused by our founding fathers have been swept aside as America works to feed the unquenchable greed of our society. America's youth are given the example that lying, fraudulent behavior, and promoting violence have become acceptable.

While some U.S. citizens have become so used to this behavior that they may find it acceptable, it is being noticed outside our borders and not favorably. The Corruption Perception Index that scores countries on a scale of 0 {highly corrupt} to 100 {very clean} has dropped the United States from a score of 76 in 2015 to 67 in 2020. We can expect a further drop in the next report. Transparency International, in assessing the corruption in the U.S., stated, "The United States is experiencing threats to its system of checks and balances and erosion of ethical norms at the highest levels of power." The system of checks and balances, as well as the separation of power, are both all but ignored by today's political leaders.

The Manhattan District Attorney filed charges against Donald Trump in a New York State criminal proceeding. District Attorney Bragg is not a federal employee. He is an elected official responsible for the enforcement of state laws. Rather than letting the criminal justice system proceed, Representative Jim Jordon demanded that the District Attorney turn over all communications, documents, and testimony to his committee. The idea that a congressional committee has a right to demand evidence in an ongoing criminal investigation of violations of state laws should have been condemned by his fellow members of Congress. Instead, D.A. Bragg had to file a lawsuit against Jordon to stop his "brazen and unconstitutional" interference and attempted obstruction. Bragg went on to call it a "transparent campaign to intimidate and attack the office of the District Attorney." To prove the claim that it was intended to intimidate D.A. Bragg, Jordon scheduled a 'field hearing' in New York City to attempt to make the case that the D.A. was ignoring serious crime to carry on the case against Trump. All these actions were a failed attempt to pressure the D. A. to drop the case against Trump. As the trial eventually began in May, a parade of Republican office holders {including the Speaker of The House} traveled to New York to interfere in the judicial process by holding press events to criticize the ongoing criminal trial. These are examples of the rampant party loyalty that President Washington warned of over two hundred years ago. The judicial branch is intended to operate completely independent of the other two branches. That is the basis of the separation of powers outlined in our constitution. It is the basis of our system of checks and balances. These basic constitutional provisions are completely ignored by the actions of these elected officials who took an oath to defend the constitution. Where is the outrage?

Jordon repeated the outrage in Fulton County, Georgia, where County District Attorney Fani Willis carried on an investigation into attempts in her state to overturn the 2020 election. The investigation resulted in charges against Trump and others under the state's RICO statute. Again, Jordon demanded evidence be turned over to him and his committee. D.A. Willis pulled no punches in her response, slamming Jordon for "interfering with an active criminal investigation." She went on to say, "There is no justification in the Constitution for Congress to interfere with a state criminal investigation. Your attempt to invoke congressional authority is flagrantly at odds with the Constitution."

All these instances are thinly disguised attempts by Congressional Republicans to obstruct criminal investigations against the sitting head of their party. It's important to note that these are state investigations conducted by state elected officials who are answerable to the people they serve, not to Congress. What's more, the system of checks and balances that has served this republic for over two hundred years relies on the separation of powers between the three branches of government. It was a key objective of James Madison, one of our founding fathers. The very idea that the blatant overreach by a member of Congress, followed by the parade of characters going to New York for the purpose of interfering with a criminal trial, was acceptable to Republicans, and that it went on without comment, or objection from them, is very disturbing. It is also further evidence of how far we have moved away from the ideals of our founding fathers. The fact that the voting public witnessed all of these actions and still chose to elect the perpetrators to control the Congress, and the Executive branch is even more disturbing. Does America no longer care about the principles and institutions upon which our nation was founded?

The disregard for the idea of separation of powers is yet another example of how the vision of our founding fathers seems to not register with the people currently in power or with the nation's electorate. It is yet another example of behavior that should inspire outrage. As a final outrageous act to take the focus away from Trump's criminal activity, House Republicans opened an impeachment investigation of President Bidden while admitting that after months of hearings, they had found no evidence of wrongdoing on the President's part. Comfortable with abusing a constitutional provision reserved by the founding fathers to be used only in the case of "high crimes and misdemeanors," they pressed on without evidence. When asked for an explanation of the action, one House Republican answered simply, "Trump 2024," in admission of the true reason for the abuse. As young students learn in their history classes of the objectives of our founding fathers they are flooded daily with examples of those principles being completely ignored by todays public elected officials.

The answer to all the questions around the lack of outrage within the country is that we have become numb to it all and that we allow it to happen and express no outrage when nothing is done about it. Judging by the results of the 2024 election the majority of citizens in the country seem not only lacking outrage, they are willing to participate in the madness. A billionaire immigrant from South Africa, whose business interests are closely tied to federal spending, was just able to assist in buying the presidency for a fellow billionaire. Elon Musk reportedly spent $250 million in support of the Trump campaign much of it spent on misleading, false advertising targeting liberals and minority voters likely to support Vice President Harris. With money exercising so much blatant influence in our process, a convicted felon as our new president, three Supreme Court Justices having lied their way on to the bench, and so much more are we now the most corrupt, immoral country on the planet? If we are not we are certainly headed in that direction. Until the American people express outrage, it will continue to get worse. Until the American people demand more integrity, more honesty, and higher moral fiber from their leaders, we will continue down this rat hole until the corruption becomes so rampant that we turn our once proud nation into the most corrupt country on earth.

> "I notice that the ceremony of your corrupt ways has finally made you blind."
>
> Bob Dylan

CHAPTER 8

THE DIVIDING OF AMERICA

There have always been divisions in America, whether between races, religions, urban and rural, liberal and conservative, rich and poor. Perhaps never since the Civil War have our divisions been as starkly defined as they are today. Divisions have peaked due to a series of presidential campaigns that attempted to capitalize on those differences and turn us against one another. In the words of Trump's own Secretary of Defense, General Mattis, "Trump is the first President in my lifetime who does not try to unite the American people. He tries to divide us." It is to the advantage of an elite, privileged class, to have the masses fighting amongst themselves.

As long as the 90% of the country that has been left disadvantaged are convinced that the root of their problems is someone or something other than the elite class at the top, there is no danger of them losing their privileged status. Throughout our history immigrants have served as a convenient scapegoat. Over the decades various nationalities coming to America have borne the brunt of this discriminatory abuse. Irish immigrants, Italian immigrants, Asian immigrants have all been subject to this kind of treatment. Today, it falls to South American immigrants coming over our southern border.

The United States has long needed an immigration policy but efforts have been stymied by our 'leaders' preferring to turn the issue into a political football. As the lack of a coherent policy to deal with the issue has dragged on a crises has developed the government continues to be unable to resolve. Consequently the situation becomes more problematic by the month as some political leaders use the issue to exaggerate the problem and spread fear that works to their political advantage. This serves to widen our divisions to the point that our political divide has now become so ingrained and so emotional that it seems impossible to imagine the two sides ever being able to work together once again for the good of the nation.

A study by Thomas Carothers and Andrew O'Donoghue concluded that "our divisions are especially multi-faceted, and there is a powerful alignment of ideology, race, and religion that renders America's divisions unusually encompassing and profound. It fuses all three types of identity divisions in a similar way." Political debates that once were ideological in nature and civil in discourse are now personal and insulting, with opposition party members being called un-American and immoral. A national poll conducted by John Zogby in 2021 found that a plurality of Americans believe we have a civil war in our future, which provides the best evidence of how dangerous our divisions have become. We have produced radical, right-wing groups like the Aryan nation and Sovereign Citizens over the years, but what makes today's situation so dangerous is that the divisions are not exclusive to radical groups. Politicians capitalizing on our fears of people's differences stoke the fires, and spread the divide.

Many of the participants in the January 6th insurrection were mainstream working Americans caught up in the claim of a liar. What's more, paramilitary groups like the Proud Boys and the Oath Keepers seized the opportunity to become relevant, and jumped into the mix fitting in nicely with the mainstream participants.

What would bring hard-working ordinary citizens to the conclusion that they need to invade the Capitol and interfere with a constitutional process? How could they be so receptive to the claims of a lifelong con man who offered no evidence to support his claim? The answer lies in decades of changes and events that have sowed distrust in our government by a large number of Americans. The instigator of the attack on the capital has been successful in riding that wave of distrust and the conspiracy theories that have deepened our divisions. He has capitalized on the fears of Americans, like the idea that there is an organized 'replacement movement' active in America with the objective of taking rights away from the white population. It is not a coincidence that the overwhelming majority of the participants in the insurrection were white males. It would be extremely naive to suggest that bigoted feelings towards people of color played no part in the insurrection and in our deepening divide. Every night, the star of Fox News, Tucker Carlson, busied himself presenting his theories of the 'polluting of American blood' by immigrants and people of color. The idea expressed by presidents as early as Washington that America should be proud of its diversity and that we should be tolerant of our differences has become unacceptable in many quarters.

It would be equally naive to believe the current wealth and income gap in our nation played no part in the insurrection. It is to the advantage of the wealthy class to spread fear and loathing among the populous. When you take away the hope from the majority of the public that they will ever get ahead economically, you are leaving them little incentive to trust in the future. The lost hope has to be replaced with another emotion, and fear works well. So we had the defeated President, the instigator of the insurrection, trying to get the presidency back by telling the nation that he would save the country. "I'm your retribution," a statement that implies that those who have been left behind can look to him for their salvation when, in reality, he has been a prime mover in the collapse of their collective futures.

Elected officials have been quoted promoting succession from the Union. Representative Marjorie Taylor Green of Georgia claimed, "We need a divorce. We need to separate by red states and blue states." Other Republican officeholders openly promote violence. Representative Madison Cawthorn of North Carolina, making the false claim of elections not being honest, said, "If our elections continue to be rigged, it's going to lead to one place, and that's bloodshed." Rep. Matt Gaetz of Florida recently commented, "Only force can make change in Washington, D.C."

Governor Rick Perry of Texas may have been joking in 2009 when he suggested Texas could succeed, but there was no joke in the 2022 Texas State Republican Convention when they accepted a platform urging the legislature to put out a referendum question to determine if the state should 're-assert its status as an independent nation.

When President Barack Obama was elected to the presidency, the Senate Republican leader declared, "It will be my job to see to it that he is a one-term president." He made this statement even before the inauguration, making it clear that there would be no Republican effort to work with the new President. This remark should have inspired outrage, but our politics have become so toxic the remark was applauded by Republicans and accepted by Democrats. It gets even worse. When the Obama administration joined with five other nations attempting to negotiate a treaty with Iran to stop that nation's nuclear program, a majority of Republican senators signed on to a letter sent to Iran's leader, basically warning Iran not to trust the United States in this matter. The Constitution gives the President the power to negotiate treaties with "the advice and consent of the Senate" —a letter that may have been considered treasonous in years past, advising a foreign government in the middle of a treaty negotiation not to trust the United States is not what is meant by advice and consent. In the meantime, the Republican House invited a leader of a foreign country who opposed the treaty to come to address a joint session of Congress to basically criticize our sitting President in his own backyard.

These are unprecedented moves that demonstrate how divided our politics have become, and these political divisions are directly related to how divided our nation has become. The constant vitriol among our 'leaders' in their political rhetoric feeds the fear and hatred in the country. We now have campaigns against woke {whatever the hell that is}, campaigns against the 'deep state' {with one presidential candidate saying he will" slit the throat of deep state employees}, campaigns against law enforcement, and the list goes on. I doubt that these types of campaigns are what the framers had in mind.

A PEW survey concluded that the differences between Republicans and Democrats on hot-button issues have widened from 15 points to 36 points in the last two decades. President Washington warned in his farewell address that intensified party spirit only leads to misery under a despotic government and a dictatorial, self-serving leader. The two political parties describe each other in ruthless characterizations that further inflame the public. The hateful descriptions of office holders with opposing views are thrown at the opposition party members and then embraced by the public. I once had a person I had just met tell me that "if you are a Democrat, you cannot be an American."

Fifty years ago, the differences between a moderate Democrat and a moderate Republican were not very great. Today, Democrats have drifted left, while

Republicans have gone so far right that they border on the authoritarian, and the two sides increasingly dislike and distrust each other. There is a complete absence of a prominent liberal Republican or a conservative Democrat. The toxicity of today's political climate has driven good public servants like Senator Olympia Snowe of Maine and Senator Mitt Romney of Utah out of the political arena.

While our political rhetoric has digressed to truly sad depths, it has been coupled with the rise of domestic terrorist groups like the Proud Boys and the Oath Keepers, who are not shy about discussing violent revolution. FBI Director Christopher Wray characterized these white supremacist groups as the greatest threat to our security as they openly advocate violence against the government. After charges were brought against Donald Trump, elected Republican officeholders have amazingly called the Justice Department and the FBI corrupt for attacking their leader. Instead of letting the system work, letting the court system decide the question of Trump's guilt, they have chosen to assail law enforcement for doing their job. Despite all the evidence that has been released to support the charges, a good segment of the population (led by Congressional Republicans) chose to believe law enforcement is corrupt rather than believing the justice system will arrive at the truth.

These attacks have served to sew distrust in our judicial system amongst many Americans. It is sad enough that the electoral process has been successfully tainted by unsubstantiated, unproven attacks. We are now seeing the same erosion of faith in our judicial system. Just as in the case of the attacks on clean elections, the attacks on the judiciary are without cause or evidence of abuse. Donald Trump claims he has done nothing wrong and is a victim, not a criminal. Rather than allowing the judicial system to hear the evidence and find the truth, the majority of the public chose to believe the accused and conclude that law enforcement and the judicial system are corrupt.

Elected officials in the Republican Party convinced then-President Nixon to resign when his guilt became obvious. Today, Republicans cling to ridiculous conspiracy theories of a corrupt system victimizing Trump in order to defend their leader whose list of indictments makes Nixon look like a boy scout. In spite of a flood of evidence giving proof of the many crimes of the former president the party chose to nominate him again for the office, and the majority of the American electorate chose to vote for him. His election has resulted in the charges pending against him being dropped providing the final nail into the claim that in America nobody is above the law. The way his former chief of staff, General Kelly put it, after all he has said and done why, would anyone think he should be president.

After questioning the legitimacy of our electoral system, casting doubts upon American institutions like law enforcement and justice officials is the next step to dealing a death blow to Democracy. When Americans no longer have confidence in elections, the rule of law, or the functioning of our government, we are ripe for the transition into autocracy. This denigration of our institutions is being promoted by and encouraged on behalf of one man whose criminal activities have taken place in plain sight of all the American people. The transition from Democracy to Oligarchy, then to Autocracy is a natural progression. Once the control of the nation has been turned over to the billionaire class the next logical step is to consolidate power in one place. Rather than three co-equal branches of government, empower the executive, and diminish the system of checks and balances. This has been the stated objective of Trump advisor Steve Bannon, and it will be a primary goal over the next four years.

So, how have things reached this stage? It did not happen overnight, but the divisions in our nation have escalated rapidly in the last eight years. The Brookings Institute conducted a survey of 300 political scientists, all members of the Political Science Association Presidents and Executive Politics section. The survey ranked the thirty most polarizing Presidents in U.S. history. President Donald Trump was ranked the number one most polarizing President by a wide margin. Even ahead of Abraham Lincoln, whose election inspired the Civil War. Respondents listed fractious Trump proposals like the travel ban, dismantling of Obama care, withdrawing from the Global Climate pact, and his praising of white supremacist groups as examples of his divisiveness. Added to this list should be his tax cut to benefit the Wealthy which widened the wealth and income gap. His rhetoric, his insulting tone, and his actions have increased the divisions in our country while at the same time increasing violence in our politics, but perhaps the greatest harm out of the Trump years has been the nation's distrust of the truth.

> ***"There will come a time when the rich own all the media. And it will be impossible for the public to make an informed Opinion."***
>
> *Albert Einstein*

The undermining of the credibility of the mainstream media has also been an ongoing process. It has developed over the years, beginning with the 'lame stream media' phrase made popular in the 80s. It has exploded in more recent years with the concept of 'fake news' popularized by Trump. Heading into the 2016 election, the British consulting firm Cambridge Analytical mined often inaccurate data from social media, re-posting it to certain audiences they deemed susceptible to the message. The Vice President of Cambridge Analytical, Steve Bannon, used these posts to promote the candidacy of Donald Trump, thus beginning the 'fake news' cycle. The Bannon posts actually were examples of fake reporting, but they were passed off as legitimate news. In order to get out in front of any criticism, they made sure to cast doubts about any legitimate news that might be critical of Trump calling such reporting "fake news." This is typical of the Trump team's strategy of accusing the opposition of doing something the Trump team is actually doing. While the Trump team would brand legitimate reporting that was unfavorable to him as 'fake news,' the real 'fake news' was appearing on blogs written by self-appointed citizen journalists who lacked any formal training in journalism and played loose with 'facts.'

Their 'reporting' found its way onto the internet, where 43% of the public now gets their news, making it increasingly difficult for trained journalists to be taken seriously. The Trump administration's desire to muddy the truth by deliberately discrediting the media and causing doubts as to what constituted the truth gave rise to non-legitimate reporting. In an interview with Lesly Stahl, a true journalist with "60 Minutes," Trump stated that "I bash the press to demean and discredit reporters so that no one will believe negative stories about me."

To accomplish this end, he has called for the boycotting of unfavorable news organizations, promoted changes in libel laws to punish those he doesn't like, and threatened regulatory action against corporate owners while continuing his bashing of the press. As the start of his second term approaches his intimidating threats are already paying dividends. A major broadcasting network, ABC, settled a law suit which Trump had filed in response to statements made by ABC anchor George Stephanopoulos, by paying $15 million as a charitable contribution to Trump's 'Presidential Foundation and Museum.' Legal experts had predicted the lawsuit was one Trump would not win but the impending Trump Presidency with its stated policy of 'going after' unfriendly news sources was enough of an intimidating factor to pay the $15 million. Fresh on the heels of that pleasant outcome the Trump team filed a lawsuit against pollster Ann Selzer and the Des Moines Register under the Iowa Consumer Fraud Act. The suit alleges that the long time pollster released a poll that she manipulated in favor of the Harris campaign in order to impact the election results against Trump. It is the first lawsuit ever filed against an opinion poll's release. Coupled with these events are reports of major newspaper owners instructing their respective editorial staffs to lay off the opinion pieces that are critical of Trump as his term of office approaches. Bullying the 'free' press is yet another practice that has become acceptable in our dormant democracy. In a classic understatement, a report from the Committee to Protect Journalists concluded that, 'Trump's attacks have dangerously undermined truth and consensus in a deeply divided country.'

The polarization of the nation has also been encouraged by media outlets outside the internet. Today, we are surrounded by misinformation from social media, as well as broadcast media organizations on radio and television, who sell themselves as "news organizations" while providing very little news. They fill the airways with opinions, misinformation, and conspiracy theories, passing it all off as news, and much of the public believes it to be legitimate. As the prophecy of Mr. Einstein has become reality, the sources of these 'news' providers are increasingly controlled be wealthy individuals with an agenda to promote. For example, the social media platform formerly known as Twitter became the property of billionaire Elon Musk who changed the name to X. Meta Platforms {including Facebook and Instagram} is owned by billionaire Mark Zuckerman and the media conglomerate that owns Fox News is owned by billionaire Robert Murdoch. None of these 'news sources' could be classified as legitimate as they all major in conspiracy theory and opinion but they are seen as legitimate by a large segment of Americans. As Albert Einstein predicted, the efforts of these wealthy owners have made finding the truth difficult. It is yet another measure of the control exercised by the wealthy class.

The segment of the population that chooses to follow the 'news' is divided into two groups (liberal/conservative), and every day, they pay attention to the broadcasts that re-assert and re-enforce what they already believe. Hateful, conspiracy theory-filled broadcasts that become more divisive every year are now not only acceptable but they are also followed religiously with little if any attention paid to opposing positions.

The "fairness doctrine" adopted in 1949 and enforced by the Federal Communications Commission mandated that news organizations broadcast fair and balanced coverage of controversial issues of interest and present the news unbiased. If they were giving an opinion, they needed to identify it as an opinion while offering equal time for opposing opinions. The origins of the doctrine lie in the Radio Act of 1927, which limited radio broadcasting to licensed broadcasters, mandating that news organizations serve the public interest. The Supreme Court upheld the doctrine in 1969's Red Lion Broadcasting Company v FCC. In the 1970s, the FCC identified the doctrine as the "single most important requirement of operation in the public interest."

The doctrine stayed in effect until the FCC in the Reagan administration, headed by Chairman Mark Fowler (a communications lawyer who served in Reagan's campaign), began rolling the application of the doctrine back. In 1987, under the new Chairman Dennis Patrick, the doctrine was repealed altogether. In June of that year, Congress passed the 'Fairness in Broadcasting Act,' which would have codified the Fairness Doctrine, but Reagan vetoed the bill. One year later, in 1988, Rush Limbaugh syndicated his conservative talk radio show chock-full of opinions and misinformation passed off as legitimate news.

It was only the beginning as hate talk broadcasting not only proliferated but simultaneously grew more outlandish as in broadcasts such as 'Infowars,' the Alex Jones Show spewing hate messaging with little basis in reality. In 1996, Rupert Murdoch's Fox News was launched, giving television a primetime purveyor of misinformation and conspiracy theories. Once again, an action coming out of the Reagan administration has had an extremely harmful long-term impact.

While all this has been brewing over the past several decades, becoming more and more divisive every year, the explosion in our divisions has come with the Trump claim of a stolen election. Still, a third of the country believes in the false claim even after seeing all the proof to the contrary. Continued support from Key Republican leaders coupled with the spread of disinformation on social media platforms and continued lies on some broadcast media channels reinforce the distrust. FOX News paid a huge fine for broadcasting what they admitted were lies about the election. They then fired the key person responsible for the falsehoods. Despite this heavy fine and the head of the network admitting to the lies broadcast on FOX, despite the firing of their liar-in-chief, viewers remain loyal to Fox while believing the lies they continue to broadcast.

The dismissal by Fox of Tucker Carlson was a step in the right direction, but the conspiracy theories and lies continue to be aired by the likes of Sean Hannity, Stuart Varney, and Laura Ingram. More than all our other differences as a nation, this false claim of election fraud has galvanized the divisions, intensifying them to a very dangerous point, all because one very narcissistic man could not admit he lost an election. His political and media allies continue to promote him as a victim even as evidence mounts of his criminal behavior. The success of all these promotions resulted in his election to the presidency in 2024. The media support coupled with the adoration he continues to receive from his fellow Republicans has put him back in power.

There has been no attempt to re-introduce the 'Fairness in Broadcasting Act' for the simple reason that it would not pass. There is so much money being made with hate talk radio and television that the misinformation in the broadcasting age is here to stay. Fox 'news' paid their huge fine out of cash flow, giving an indication of the money to be made with these types of lies. The station continues to pass along misinformation and outright lies while making so much money at it that another lawsuit is of no concern.

Safeguards have been built into our system of government, and they worked after the 2020 elections. Our checks and balances and the rule of law stymied the attempted coup by Trump and his cronies. However, will we find in the future that the actions in the 2020 election aftermath, was simply a dress rehearsal that served to identify the weaknesses? Changes have already been put in place to make it easier in a future attempt to subvert the will of the electorate.

In a second term, Trump would make sure to surround himself with supporters who will not stand in his way, even if he acts illegally. There will be no restraints in a second Trump term or in a future term by another MAGA candidate. Does that indicate we are on the verge of a transition from an oligarchy to autocracy?

> *"One of the saddest lessons of history is this: if we've been bamboozled long enough, we tend to reject any evidence of the bamboozle. We're no longer interested in finding out the truth. The bamboozle has captured us. It's simply too painful to acknowledge, even to ourselves, that we've been taken. Once you give a charlatan power over you, you almost never get it back."*
>
> *Carl Sagan*

CHAPTER 9

AMERICA'S CHANGING GLOBAL IMAGE

"Unfortunately, President Trump did not grow to match the office. His smallness has instead diminished it. The American President has long served as a model for the nation, but few would imagine holding Donald Trump up for their children to emulate. Around the world, he and, to some degree, the nation that elected him has become a laughingstock. His poverty of character has been exposed so often and in so many ways that many here have become inured to it. Not so for those who watch from abroad."

Senator Mitt Romney

DEMOCRACY

When I first read those words of Senator Romney I was reminded of a scene at an international event during the first Trump Administration. A camera caught the leaders of France, Great Britain, and Germany in a group discussing our President and laughing at his incompetence. It was an embarrassing scene for the United States. The Biden Administration has worked for the past four years to strengthen the NATO alliance. Much to the consternation of Vladimir Putin, Sweden and Finland joined the alliance at the urging of the United States. We have supplied money and arms to Ukraine in the war with Russia. As we approach the second Trump term our allies in Europe indicated they can no longer count on the support of the United States in NATO or in the war against Russia. The prospects for our allies today are not a laughing matter.

The United States of America has been the beacon of democracy around the world for centuries. That image has suffered greatly in the past eight years, and while the total blame for this can't be placed on Donald Trump, he has certainly been the major factor. As much a factor as his own actions as president has been the influence he has had in setting the Republican Party in the 'America first' direction, which has been equally to blame. Our allies around the world who have looked to the leadership of the U.S. for years no longer express confidence in America.

A survey carried out a year after the first Trump administration by the Latina polling company, commissioned by the Alliance of Democracies Foundation, interviewed fifty thousand respondents in fifty-three countries. The findings demonstrate the problems the U.S. now has in presenting itself as the standard of democracy or as the protector of democracies worldwide. The pole identified economic inequality as the biggest threat to democracy even as America drifted further and further away from the New Deal policies that brought economic equality to the nation. Democracy stands for equality and freedom, but these are hollow principles if the government is unable to create circumstances for all citizens to obtain basic needs. Surveys reveal that many feel democracy is inadequately addressing the socio-economic problems associated with globalization. While the poll found strong support for democracy worldwide, it also found that 44% of respondents were concerned that the decline in American democracy threatens the existence of democracy in their own country.

What's more, respondents identified the U.S. as a bigger threat to democracy than China or Russia {44% for the U.S., 38% for China, and 28% for Russia}. The polling company attributed the findings to a 'hangover effect of the Trump America first foreign policy.' With the results of our recent election the 'hangover' has become more severe has the rest of the world seems more concerned about the demise of our democracy than does our own electorate.

Majorities in many European countries think the U.S. political system is broken and unable to function. While they rejoiced when Biden was elected over

Trump, most Europeans don't believe he can bring American stature back to its former greatness. With the second coming of Trump their fears have been heightened. Many feel they can no longer rely on American leadership or protection and now see Germany as their most important ally. Newspapers across Europe have written that America can no longer lay claim to being a beacon of democracy or impose electoral standards on other countries.

The head of the FBI has stated repeatedly that the biggest threats for violence in America come from within the country, not from without. Opinion polling shows that those asked to identify the threats to democracy see the biggest threats coming from within. This is true in America as well as with other Western European democracies. Confidence in political institutions, as well as political parties, has plummeted not only in the U.S. but with many of our allies. Hungary and Poland have both witnessed a weakening of their democracies in terms of their independent civil society and the rule of law, as strong leaders have introduced authoritarian policies to replace more democratic principles. Not surprisingly, Trump praises these strong-armed leaders who have managed to circumvent their own democracies. He holds them up as models of the America he envisions. The America he will work to shape over the next four years.

Concerns and criticisms of the state of democracy in America are not restricted to our European allies; less friendly nations have expressed their delight in what they describe as an American democracy in decline. Russian news has been full of stories about the chaos in America. After the insurrection on January 6th, Russian television gleefully showed scenes from the Capital riots, seeing them as evidence of American decline. Russian broadcasts made the claim that the 'archaic out of date' electoral system and deep divides in the country had left "American democracy limping on both feet." The Moscow Times wrote that the "celebration of democracy has ended" and America has hit rock bottom.

The People's Republic of China's Ministry of Foreign Affairs issued their analysis in March of 2023. The report begins by saying, "The vicious cycle of democratic pretensions, dysfunctional politics, and divided society continued in America in 2022". The report goes on to describe a nation with its democracy in decline, a population increasingly disillusioned with democracy, and political polarization intensified by partisan fights. The re-election of Trump to the office of President has been celebrated in these countries that have a history of unfriendly relations with America while our allies have reacted with trepidation. It should serve as a disturbing signal to Americans that our allies see Trump's election as cause for deep concern, while our traditional enemies see it as a cause for celebration.

While one would not expect a glowing assessment of America by the Russians or the Chinese, it is difficult to argue with their analysis, given the state of things today. Our adversaries receive our partisan disputes, coupled with the flood of anti-democratic initiatives and the inflammatory rhetoric from many of our politicians, with great delight. We have even witnessed U. S. political figures parroting Russian propaganda lines again to the delight of our adversaries. In some cases political figures who have echoed Russian propaganda have been suggested to be members of a Trump cabinet.

CHAPTER 10

WHERE ARE WE HEADED FROM HERE

TRUMP ALLEGIANCE IS BAFFLING

He criticized and degraded John McCain a true American Hero. He said he didn't want to be seen with combat veteran amputees because it did not look good for him. He called our fallen heroes who lost their lives defending our country "suckers and losers" while refusing to visit their graves in Normandy because it was raining. Most recently he desecrated the sacred ground at Arlington National Cemetery for a cheap campaign photo. He and V.P. candidate Vance participated in crafting project 2025 which calls for a reduction in veteran's benefits and the closing of several V.A. hospitals. Yet when he talks about his support for our men and women in uniform you chose to believe him and conclude that General Kelly, General Mattis, and other decorated combat veterans are liars. Only Trump speaks the truth.

He mocked a disabled reporter for cheap laughs and even though you saw it with your own eyes you don't believe it happened because he says he didn't do it. You saw him incite an insurrection on live television, but now he says the thugs that destroyed property, beat police officers, defecated and urinated in the halls of our capital are patriots and you believe that as well. He has been indicted by four different Grand Juries in four different states, convicted in civil court of molesting a woman, plus found guilty of fraud on three occasions. He has been convicted of thirty four felonies by a prosecutor, and jury completely unconnected to the Department of Justice yet you believe him when he says he has done nothing wrong, and this is all Joe Biden 'weaponizing' the justice system. The twelve jurors who convicted him were ordinary citizens jointly chosen by the prosecutor and Trump's high priced attorneys. All the defense attorneys had to do was get one of the twelve not to vote to convict yet after hearing the evidence the vote to convict was unanimous thirty four times. Yet you still think he has done nothing wrong.

Perhaps the worst thing he has done is to cast doubts among many Americans about the validity of our electoral process and the rule of law. With zero proof he has convinced you that the election was rigged. This has left a large segment of the population doubting the honesty of the process, a process that has been renowned worldwide as the fairest, most honest electoral process on the planet. FOX news paid a huge fine for joining in on the lie admitting under oath that they lied. Rudy Giuliani also admitted under oath that he lied but you continue to believe the election was stolen simply because Trump says so.

As you continue to support and vote for this man even as the convictions pile up and his project 2025 agenda threatens an end to our democracy think of the example he is setting for the youth of America. Perhaps you will be able to think of a way to explain to your own children and grandchildren why you supported such a man. They will probably ask the question as they see the ideals upon which our country was founded disappearing.

TAKEN FROM A LETTER TO THE EDITOR

So, the high ideals of our founding fathers, the hallmarks of our first President, are under siege. The work of President Roosevelt to create a prosperous middle class and a sound financial system is also under attack. The efforts of President Lincoln to hold together a divided country seem to be needed again, as we are as divided a nation as at any time since Lincoln. Our once precious democracy has been gradually transformed into an oligarchy controlled by the wealthy. Once the electoral process and the wheels of power have been turned over to the small wealthy class at the top, the next logical step is to transition from an Oligarchy to Autocracy. This has all come about over the past forty years. It has happened so gradually that the outrage that should be present among the population has been slow to form. As bad as all that seems it is about to get much, much worse.

On November 5th, 2024 Donald Trump was elected to a second four year term of office. He was elected in spite of all his outrages actions, all the criminal charges, and all his hate filled rhetoric fueling our divisions. He was elected with a solid majority giving him a mandate to advance his agenda. In addition, he was rewarded with a Republican majority in the Congress and, of course, immunity for any criminal actions as granted by our corrupt Supreme Court. He has vowed to surround himself with staff, and advisors that are totally loyal to him and his agenda. To that end he has offered a list of highly controversial potential cabinet members that will test the mettle of the Senate. Where we go from here will depend on the remaining strength of our democratic institutions after forty plus years of their gradual demise, and whether there exists enough courage in the Republican controlled Senate to stand up to Donald Trump.

DEMOCRACY

The early resistance to Trump's demand that the Congress adjourn to allow recess appointments was encouraging. However, Trump has dispatched his enforcer, Elon Musk, to the hill in order to threaten and intimidate Senate members who have expressed concern over his very unqualified recommendations for cabinet appointments. Recalcitrant Senators are being threatened with primary opponents funded by Musk's PAC if they continue their obstinate behavior, yet another example of money controlling our elected officials. Republican members of the Senate, fearful of losing their positions of power, are already shamefully caving to the pressure applied by Musk even as the Trump recommendations for key positions become more outrages. This is what we have come to, a billionaire immigrant bullying, and threatening our elected officials. Is this what the American people wanted? Is this what they voted for November fifth?

- For Attorney General Trump has offered up the name of Florida Congressman Matt Gaetz. Geatz has been under investigation by the ethics committee for having sexual relations with a minor and was formerly investigated by the FBI for sex trafficking. A controversial pick, so unpopular with Republican Senators, that his name was withdrawn and replaced with another Trump loyalist, former Florida Attorney General Pam Bondi, a former lobbyist for a foreign country making her also a controversial pick. While Bondi has the experience that Gaetz lacked, her main qualification is loyalty to Trump which she demonstrated by refusing to bring an action against Trump University in the state of Florida. To serve in the top two positions supporting Attorney General Bondi Trump has offered his defense council Todd Blanche, and Emil Bove. Again, while they are both experience prosecutors their main qualification is loyalty to Trump, and a willingness to do whatever Trump tells them.

Trump decided he would offer one more controversial selection suggesting his pick for FBI director would

DEMOCRACY

be Trump loyalist Kash Patel. Current FBI director Christopher Wray cleared one of the hurdles to Patel's appointment by announcing he would resign effective at the end of the Biden administration. He was originally appointed by then President Trump in 2017. To replace him with Patel Trump is signaling that the agency will be in business to carry out Trump's vendetta against his perceived enemies. In addition, Patel has made noise about criminalizing his own grievances around the activities of the 'deep state' while making no bones about his support for Trump's efforts to 'go after' his political opponents. In a recent action by the House Republicans the table has been set for Patel to 'go after' Trump's chief protagonist, Liz Cheney. A report authored by Representative Loudermilk contained a fabricated case of witness tampering centered around a claim Cheney met with a key witness coming before the January 6th committee, without the witnesses lawyer present, in order to shape her testimony. There appears to be little evidence to support the charge but the letter from the Laudermilk committee requesting an investigation awaits the appointment of Patel to take charge of the request. This all makes him a third controversial appointment in the law enforcement field. The trifecta of Attorney General Bondi {supported by Trump's defense attorneys}, FBI director Patel, and director of intelligence agencies {including the CIA} Tulsi Gabbard all pledging loyalty to Trump, presents a scary scenario.

- For Secretary of Homeland Security Kristi Noem the Governor of South Dakota a position in which she has gained zero experience that would qualify her for the job. Like the other suggested cabinet members, her main qualification is her loyalty to Trump.

- As Director of National Intelligence Tulsi Gabbard an officer in the Army Reserve. A former Democratic Congress Woman from Hawaii she is viewed with suspicion by a number of Senators for various reasons including her suspected connections to Russia. She was also viewed with suspicion by TSA security. TSA had her on a flight watch list because of her suspicious foreign travel.

- As Secretary of Defense Pete Hegseth also a member of the National Guard. Hegseth has been suspected by fellow Guard members of having 'radical' views. His choice is based on his performance as a Fox News commentator which of course provides no experience for the job. Senators from both parties have expressed concern about his lack of qualifications for such an important position. His nomination would be further burdened by a California police report detailing a 2017 allegation of sexual assault, and reports of his problems with alcohol.

- Robert F Kennedy Jr. as Secretary of Health and Human Services. Kennedy would oversee the Nation's most important health organizations even as he comes to the job with little training in the field of medicine and health. His long standing adamant opinions on health issues like vaccines is troubling for many in the health field. Equally troubling in this area is the suggestion of Mehmet Oz {doctor Oz} to oversee the Medicare/Medicaid programs. As a television personality Oz offered medical advice 40% of which were found lacking in any scientific bases by Canadian researchers'. Finally as the head of the National Institutes of Health he proposes Stanford University professor of health policy Jay Bhattacharya. In this position Bhattacharya will have significant influence on the direction of medical research in America. His opposition to the COVID precautions including his skepticism of the effectiveness of the COVID vaccine make many in the health field leery of his appointment. Just as in the area of the proposed justice appointments, the proposed trifecta of Kennedy, Oz, and Bhattacharya causes concern in the health field.

- During the campaign candidate Trump professed to have no knowledge of the controversial Project 2025. He claimed repeatedly that he had no connection to it yet he has proposed Russell Vought to head the Office of Management and Budget. Vought is the main architect of Project 2025.

- He proposes professional wrestling founder Linda McMahon as the Secretary of Education. McMahon once lied about having a degree in Education in applying for membership on a board of education. She has no such educational background.

- For the newly formed Department of Government Efficiency Trump proposes two of his billionaire friends Elon Musk and Vivek Ramaswany. Between them the pair has absolutely zero experience in the workings of the government. Having these two wealthy individuals, with no experience in the effectiveness of 'safety net' programs in relieving hunger and poverty, taking a hatchet to the federal budget is a disturbing prospect.

These are just a few of Trump's suggested cabinet members and they all have two things in common;

- They have pledged absolute loyalty to Trump and vowed to follow his orders to the letter and

- They possess little if any experience or expertise in the areas they are potentially going to be in charge of running.

To a person these appointments are intended to give the new President carte blanche to do whatever he chooses with no checks on his actions even if they are criminal in nature. To those who cling to the idea that constitutional safeguards will protect the country, the reality is that our Supreme Court has rendered those safeguards much less effective. The willingness of the majority of the Court to fall in line behind the 'legal strategies' of the Trump team make enforcement of constitutional norms very suspect. How, for example, will this Court rule when the administration impounds money authorized by Congress because the expenditures would be contrary to the wishes of the Musk, Ramaswamy team? It is a very safe bet that the Trump administration will be challenging the authority of the other branches to exercise their roles in the 'checks and balances' of government whenever their actions interfere with his agenda. Those challenges will eventually end up in front of a Supreme Court that has demonstrated its own loyalty to Trump.

In order to provide the Congress with forewarning of the limited role they will play in the new administration, he suggested the Senate should allow 'recess appointments' to these positions. The transition team is also not bothering with the traditional FBI background checks for cabinet nominees. This is intended to demonstrate right from the start that in the Trump administration the Congress, as well as law enforcement, will be as subservient to the new leader as will be his cabinet members. There has been initial resistance to these demands by Republican Senators who have stated they intend to fulfill their constitutional role in the confirmation process. Add to that the recent statement from the Republican Senator form Alaska,

Lisa Murkowski that she will not confirm any appointments without the required FBI background checks. The initial resistance is encouraging to those who seek to preserve our system of checks and balances, but the question will be whether or not it will last. Will the Senate decide not to confirm the most controversial nominees like Kennedy, Gabbard, and Hegseth? That decision will be up to the Republican majority who control the Senate. It will be an early indicator of the Senates ability to stand up to the Trump efforts at total control. If the Senate Republicans don't have the backbone to stand up to Trump {and Musk} in the confirmation process larger challenges to their role will be surely coming from the Trump administration. At the end of his first term he expressed his own interpretation of the 'Impoundment Control Act' stating that the President has complete discretion when it comes to actually spending the money Congress has authorized. This would be in direct conflict to the constitutional provisions giving Congress the 'power of the purse'. We can expect Musk led attempts to impound funds in violation of the Act and the constitution while encouraging challenges to the administration's actions being decided by the friendly Supreme Court.

The intelligence offices have always been viewed with skepticism by Trump, and the appointment of Gabbard as director will be viewed with skepticism by a larger audience. The fear will be that intelligence agencies in our allied countries will be reluctant to share information with the U. S. because of the new directors history with Russian propaganda. Kennedy's radical views on vaccines, while extremely disturbing, are only the tip of the iceberg when it comes to the concerns of the medical and scientific communities. The idea of him overseeing the health departments of the country with his lack of qualifications coupled with a radical agenda constitutes the most concerning of the potential appointments. The lack of background for Noem, Musk, and Ramaswamy are of great concern particularly when one listens to the saber-rattling of Musk. In the end the list of names makes clear that the direction in all areas will come from

Trump himself with little to no room for input, or disagreement form other quarters.

Republican Presidents since Reagan have been guided by the 'Mandates for Leadership' issued every four years by the Heritage Foundation. Over the four plus decades of this practice the 'Mandates' have become increasingly more radical. The advantages provided for the wealthy by the implementation of the Heritage Foundation's agendas coupled with the loosening of reporting requirements for contributions has resulted in millions of dollars from 'dark money' contributors going to the Heritage Foundation increasing their strength yearly. Yet another example of the control money exercises in our system.

The 'Mandate for Leadership' issued for the 2024 election was written by, and guided by MAGA loyalists and supported by Trump and his advisors in spite of his denials. The agenda that it provides for implementation by our new, unchecked, President is the most radical offering yet. 'Project 2025'is a thirty chapter, 920 page document which spells out the path by which the progression from democracy to oligarchy to autocracy will be completed.

No place in 'Project 2025' or in any Republican candidate's campaign rhetoric is there discussion of changing an economy that caters to the wealthy, restoring voting rights, or getting money out of our political system so elected officials can act on behalf of the citizens instead of special interests. No place in the 'Mandate' is their discussion of addressing climate change, the national debt, improving our global image, restoring the money stolen from the Social Security System or the fact that billionaires pay taxes at a lower rate than working people. Instead it intends to replace our current government with a type of Christian Authoritarianism that will "rescue the country from woke cultural warriors." The language and goals contained in Project 2025 mirror very closely the rhetoric of candidate Trump. With his obvious intention to govern with total control we can expect he will work to the enactment of Project 2025 goals. The reach of 'Project 2025' is extensive covering a number of area's that can be broken down;

CITIZENS RIGHTS

The issue that gains the most attention is the right for women to control their own bodies in terms of reproductive freedom. That right was taken from them in many states after the Supreme Court struck down the Roe decision. With the new administration that may be only the beginning. The Affordable Care Act provides that most private insurance plans provide coverage for preventive birth control methods without copayments. This will be at risk with the agenda of 2025 along with the use of birth control in general as the plan calls for replacing the Department of Health and Human Services with the Department of Life. Members of the Trump team have openly discussed a national ban on abortion meaning that type of medical care will not be available anywhere in the country. Trump's appointment of Kennedy means the department will be headed by a director who has changed his stance

DEMOCRACY

on the issue and stated openly his support for a national abortion ban.

In addition the "project" calls for eliminating LGBQ rights including, marital rights, and the elimination of transgender rights. It would also eliminate funding for Diversity Equality Inclusion {DEI} programs. Participation in any such program or in critical race theory will result in dismissal for government employees. This is all part of their "war on woke." Trump has spoken of eliminating the Department of Education which provides states with important statistical data as well as money for things like support for handicapped students. Trump claims the department promotes 'woke' curriculums ignoring the fact that curriculum decisions are made at the state level. The attempts to re-write history in order to remove historical events the MAGA team find troubling will certainly continue.

There is no mention in 'Project 2025' of restoring voting rights but there is talk about redefining religious rights. The government would be charged with defining religious values for the purpose of shaping policy. Obviously this will put a number of religions at risk in a Christian Authoritarian Country.

GOVERNMENT REGULATIONS

Trump has made it clear that in the new administration all key departments will be under his direct control from the White House. That would include the Federal Communications Commission {FCC}. One of the key elements of an authoritarian government is the dispensing of propaganda. Hitler had his propaganda ministry headed by Joseph Goebbels. Since the elimination of the 'Fairness Doctrine' propaganda in the United States has been handle by a number of diverse but effective sources. Instead of a central ministry of propaganda, in the U.S. propaganda has been dispensed by sources on the left and the right using social media, as well as broadcast media. The system is just as full of untruths and false conspiracy theory as was the Goebbels operation and both sides, liberal and conservative, listen to the sources that say what they want to hear. This has been a primary cause of the divisions in America.

The next logical step for an authoritarian leader is to silence the voices against his agenda. That is precisely what Trump has talked of doing. He has openly discussed punishing news agencies that publish/broadcast unkind stories about him. He suggests lawsuits against the Corporate heads of such agencies or interfering with their licensing, even using the Internal Revenue Services to wreak havoc with their operations. As a sign of things to come, just the threat of such actions convinced the Washington Post not to endorse a candidate for president in 2024 under fear of reprisal.

He would also control the Security and Exchange Commission {SEC}. Remember that Stock Buy Backs became legal during the Reagan administration, one can only imagine the innovative initiatives that the Trump advisors can dream up to make it even easier for the wealthy to manipulate the stock market.

Environmental regulations would also be on the block. There will be a major rollback in addressing climate change as the 'project' calls for shutting down the office of Domestic Climate Policy. In addition it calls for the closing of the National Oceanic and Atmospheric Administration even as hurricanes are becoming more frequent and more severe. Also gone will be the Office of Environmental Justice, and the Energy office of Clean Energy Demonstrations. Basically, environmental concerns will be left up to Corporate America to address. What could go wrong?

Trump has even talked of taking control of the Federal Reserve. This department is responsible for controlling interest rates which they will adjust in order to address economic issues in the country. They traditionally raise interest rates in times of high inflation, and lower them to address a sluggish economy. No sitting president is ever happy to see interest rates rise, because it is very unpopular with business and consumers. To avoid political influence the Reserve has always been independent and the seven members of the board serve fourteen year staggered terms to maintain independence. Trump has stated that he wants control of the Federal Reserve to be in the White House in his administration. This would have devastating consequences for the economy as the main tool for controlling inflation is placed in jeopardy.

JUSTICE AND LAW ENFORCEMENT

Perhaps the most disturbing area that will lose its independence and come under the direct control of the White House is the Justice Department. The 'Project' calls for a complete overhaul of the FBI and the placing of the previously independent Justice Department along with the newly structured FBI under the control of the President. In fact, all federal law enforcement would come under the control of the President. In addition Homeland Security would also be restructured with law enforcement capabilities to address immigration as a priority. With the suggested appointment of Pam Bondi as Attorney General, Kristi Noem as Secretary of

Homeland Security and Tulsi Gabbard overseeing the CIA Trump will have complete control. Imagine the entire federal law enforcement and intelligence staff under the direct control of Donald Trump. What could go wrong?

CONTROL OF FEDERAL EMPLOYEES

Donald Trump learned in his first administration that having people around him that would not obey his commands would make it difficult for him to achieve his goals. There were good reasons why forty of his closest advisors in his first administration did not support his re-election. Beyond his Cabinet and close advisors civil servants at all levels of the bureaucracy {the deep state as he called it} that do not share his vision of the world create obstacles that will be eliminated in the second administration.

For months leading up to the election a team of Trump supporters worked to create a stable of potential candidates for employment in a Trump administration. This data base of personnel was vetted to ensure loyalty to 'conservative values' and to Trump himself. The 'Project' calls for the newly minted President, upon taking office, to dismiss tens of thousands of civil servants replacing them with candidates chosen from the group previously vetted. In this hiring process, just as in the selection of potential cabinet members, competency will not be of any importance. All that counts is the loyalty to Trump. These new employees will serve at the pleasure of our new President. They will have been trained in the 'Presidential Training Academy', and will take office knowing their role is to eliminate 'harmful policy/programs' under the guidance of their leader.

The long standing practice of qualifications for employment including civil service exams will fall by the wayside as Trump reshapes the government in his image. Any idea of checks and balances will be replaced by executive control. His cabinet as well as lower level positions will be filled with unqualified lackeys who will be required to swear loyalty to Trump and his agenda.

ELIMINATION OF MIDDLE CLASS SAFETY NET PROGRAMS

Trickle-down economics coupled with the huge tax breaks for wealthy citizens and corporations has not done enough damage to the middle class in the opinion of the Heritage Foundation. The 'project' calls for more tax cuts at the highest income levels, and an additional $500 billion cut in the corporate tax. What also needs to be done to further cripple the lower 90% of the country is to eliminate a number of federal programs that benefit the poor and middle class. The team of Elon Musk and Vivek Ramaswamy, have promised 'trillions of dollars' in cuts to the federal budget. Thus, a number of federal expenditures are at risk of severe cutbacks or elimination;

- Programs designed to address hunger and food shortages like the Supplemental Nutrition Assistance Program {SNAP] and the Nutrition Program for Women, Infants and

Children {WIC} are at risk for major cutbacks in funding.

- Housing programs such as Section 8 vouchers put in place to address housing needs for the poor will be reduced, this at a time when the country is facing a housing shortage.

- Health programs like Medicaid and Children's Health Insurance {CHIP} will face funding challenges. In addition efforts to lower drug prices by having government health programs negotiate prices will be at risk. Placating big Pharma will require past successful efforts at lowering prices such as the fixing of the price of insulin, to be rolled back.

- The Child Tax Credit a major economic support program for middle class America is at risk. The Head Start Program that provides early education for children of low income families is also at risk.

- The 'Project' calls for a simplified income tax with just two brackets. Analysts have predicted the adjusted brackets couple with the recommended elimination of a number of middle class friendly deductions will result in a TAX INCREASE FOR THE MIDDLE CLASS. As if a tax increase were not enough to further cause pain to American workers they propose to allow employers to avoid paying overtime.

VETERANS AFFAIRS

Project 2025 calls for a number of changes in medical care for our veterans and none of them are good. First they propose to privatize healthcare for veterans placing V A hospitals in a for-profit system. It proposes cost savings that might be achieved by targeting disability ratings of veterans. This has the potential of causing disabled veterans to lose benefits. Specialized care for veterans would be under review with the review process being handled not by people with expertise but by examiners loyal to the Trump agenda. What could possibly go wrong with such a system.

OUR ROLE IN WORLD AFFAIRS

- America's role in world affairs would be dramatically altered. No longer will our traditional allies be able to look to The United States for support. No longer will we be the beacon of democracy to the world, the protector of freedoms and liberty. As for the war in the Ukraine, in Trump's own words "Russia can do whatever the hell it wants to do." The NATO treaty is at risk of losing its American partner as we embark on a policy of adoration for dictators and weakness in dealing with countries that threaten world peace.

All of this is combined with economic objectives espoused by Trump that contain dangers of their own. He has talked of a 20% tariff on all imports with no apparent understand that the result will be increased prices for American consumers. His deportation rhetoric, if carried out could have the effect of causing labor shortages in key areas of farm production. Both initiatives hold the potential to bring inflationary pressure to the economy. If Trump is successful in taking control of the Federal Reserve Board the traditional tool to combat inflation may not even be available. The effect of all of these drastic changes is the creation of uncertainty as to our future. Nothing dampens enthusiasm for investment, and creates more volatility in the financial sector than uncertainty. Wall Street firms predicted during the campaign for president that the Trump economic agenda if enacted would result in a recession. Only time will tell if their prediction was accurate.

In his book, THE CONSPIRACY TO END AMERICA, long-time Republican strategist Stuart Stevens lists the five ways his old party is driving the American democracy to autocracy. He states in the book that the Republican Party has "become an autocratic movement masquerading as a political party" and that the current 'corrupt system' is something he, as a Republican strategist, helped to construct. I can't argue with him on either of those points. The five autocratic building blocks he listed that are necessary to drive us to autocracy;

- Propagandists- the social media and broadcast media operating with no journalistic rules, see facts as irrelevant and spread propaganda. This is just the appropriate formula of misinformation.

- It needs the support of a major party. The 2000 Republican convention developed no platform other than a pledge of loyalty and support for Trump. The Republican National Committee censured Elizabeth Chaney and Matt Kinzinger for their opposition to Trump. Congressional Republicans still support the 'big lie' even knowing it's a lie. There is no viable alternative within the Republican Party to obedient support for Trump.

- It requires money. Financier's Money continues to flow to election deniers even as their support of the lie threatens democracy.

The wealth of people like Elon Musk appears to be at the disposal of the MAGA movement.

- It requires legal theories to legitimize actions. We see this around the January 6th insurrection. Trump and his followers continue to downplay the insurrection with alternative accounts and theories of what happened that day.

- The final ingredient he sees as Shock Troops. Again, as seen in the January 6th insurrection with the participation of the proud boys and the oath keepers, Shock Troops are involved. All five of these areas, as well as other factors, have been discussed at length in this book. The bottom line is that we can all agree that the movement is well underway to bring authoritarian rule to the world's longest standing democracy. The shift to an Oligarchy was gradual taking forty years to complete, the shift from Oligarchy to Autocracy will happen quickly. We can also agree that Trump is the leader of this movement. However, it will not change if Trump is gone because he has so successfully molded the Republican Party in his image. Even without his presence MAGA will continue for years. While I agree with and am encouraged by all the attention and concern for the demise of democracy today, it is unfortunate that the movement from democracy to Oligarchy started by the Reagan Revolution did not attract as much concern. Perhaps if the transition to Oligarchy had met with more resistance we could have avoided the current state of affairs.

Donald Trump told us at every campaign stop that he intends to turn the country into an autocratic state. The Heritage Foundation has put that goal in print with Project 2025, and Governor DeSantis has given us proof that the goal is ingrained in the Republican Party. The State of Florida has provided a glimpse of the America we may be living in as Republicans take control after the 2024 election. In Florida a dictator determines what is appropriate to be taught in schools while dismissing teachers who fail to knuckle under to his education edicts. Long lists of 1,406 banned books, health care options limited by the government, and attacks by the central government against those who dare to express any disagreement with the 'ruler,' {as in the DeSantis' attack on Disney World}. Things in Florida have even reached the point of firing an elected District Attorney because the 'ruler' does not like the prosecutorial performance. The leadership style indicates that the power of the government is to be used to exact vengeance on your opponent rather than to serve the public. As distasteful as the actions in Florida may be, the latest 'mandate for leadership' manifesto from the Heritage Foundation, PROJECT 2025, is far more foreboding. As long as the Republican Party takes it's guidance from the Heritage Foundation we will never again see a Republican like Dwight Eisenhower.

The majority of the nation chose to not only believe the lie that the 2020 election was stolen but to further believe that a person charged with 91 felony counts by four different Grand Juries in 4 different parts of the country has done nothing wrong and is a victim, not a criminal. Trump supporters push the theory that his legal problems stem from President Biden's 'weaponizing' of the Justice Department. In this theory, they ignore the fact that indictments in New York and Georgia were issued by locally elected District Attorneys not working in the Justice Department. They chose to ignore his conviction of thirty four felony counts by a jury of twelve ordinary citizens chosen jointly by the prosecution and Trump's own defense attorneys. All the defense had to do was to get one juror to vote not to convict, just one, but the verdict was unanimous thirty four times. The reality is that if the head of the Justice Department, Attorney General Merrick Garland, had taken the actions against Trump years earlier as he should have, Trump could well be facing jail time rather than a term as President. The selection of Garland, a terribly weak leader as Attorney General may well have been President Biden's biggest mistake.

Also ignored is the fact that all the indictments were approved in the Grand Jury process in four different states. They ignored the fact that Trump has been convicted of fraud several times, as well as his conviction for sexually molesting a woman. In voting him into the presidency his supporters ignored the warnings of a dozen Generals and a dozen former Secretaries of Defense that he posed a threat to national security. They ignored the warning of his former Chief of Staff, General John Kelly that Trump fit the classic definition of a Fascist.

Donald Trump has proposed eliminating the Constitution, investigating news agencies that he does not like, and charging them with treason. He proposes to bring criminal charges against owners and executives of news agencies he considers unfriendly. He talks openly about seeking vengeance against all who oppose him. He has called for the execution of a retiring, highly decorated Army General who dared to cross him. All of this was disclosed to the public yet they voted Trump into the highest office in the land. As difficult as that is to understand it is the case, and it will shape where we are headed as a nation.

Perhaps it can be explained why the general public could look past all of Trumps issues, but why were these outrages not enough for elected members of his party to turn away from him. After the insurrection many elected Republican officials who had run for their lives away from the mob attacking the capital spoke out. Kevin McCarthy the leading House Republican, and Republican Senate leader Mitch McConnell were amongst that group to speak against Trump. They had their chance to get rid of him as the vote to convict was before them after the House impeachment vote. Sadly the vote to convict fell three votes short and Trump's former critics all rallied around him within a month of the vote.

Over the time Trump was standing trial for his actions Judges and prosecutors and their families have been subjected to threats. More security has been necessary for judicial personnel and their families than at any time during the prosecution of organized crime figures. Trump's calls to violence have been adopted in broad circles within the Republican Party. The nomination of Congressman

Jordon to the position of Speaker of the House resulted in death threats to members of his own party who opposed his nomination. Threats were made not only to fellow members of Congress but to their families. Threats and intimidation are now a major part of political strategy for Republican office seekers. Yet all of this seems acceptable as we move into an autocracy. Perhaps it is what the American people want. Violence and the threat of violence will now be standard fare in our political system. On the day of the most recent election there were multiple bomb threats around the country at polling places in heavily democratic areas. This was an obviously organized plan to intimidate voters in these areas, and discourage turnout. This type of behavior has all come about as Trump has reshaped the Republican Party and indeed the country.

All the elected republicans up and down the ballot seem ready to adopt the Heritage Foundation's mandate for leadership that will put us on a fast track to authoritarian rule. Indeed, the manifesto seems to be perfectly acceptable in all Republican circles especially to Trump's MAGA group. Every American should read the project 2025 manifesto from the Heritage Foundation. Their repeated 'mandates for leadership' have become more at odds with the visions of the founders of our democracy with every version.

The Project 2025 plan calls for the massive transfer of authority to the executive branch. It calls for dramatically weakening our system of checks and balances among co-equal branches of government. It eliminates tens of thousands of civil service positions and replaces them with political appointments that will be answerable to and loyal to the President. The plan looks to weed out the areas of the executive branch that have not been supportive of the MAGA agenda. The Justice Department will be the legal arm of the administration, again answerable only to the president.

An equally disturbing aspect of the new administration concerns the nations Federal Court system. All judicial appointments would continue to come from the Federalist Society's list of qualified candidates. The Courts role as an independent player in a system of checks and balances has been severely damaged and is on the verge of being completely lost. Implementation of Project 2025 will be the end of any hope of returning to the democracy on which this country was founded. The system of checks and balances, so crucial to the founders, will essentially no longer exist as the Courts lose their independence and become simply another partisan political organization. Any doubt that this will be the ultimate result have been erased by the Supreme Court's ruling on the question of Presidential immunity. Trump will achieve his stated goal of 'suspending the constitution' by further packing the high Court with 'Justices' that will do his bidding. As we contemplate all of this, we need to remember that this country was founded on the basic principles of liberty, freedom of speech, freedom of religion, due process of law, and freedom of assembly. We have existed for centuries as a nation built on the rule of law. How do the stated goals of the Trump administration, as well as Project 2025, fit with these founding principles? How can any patriotic American not be completely outraged by the blatant disregard of our nation's heritage?

The song 'A Day in The Life' recorded by the Beatles more than fifty years ago put to music the busy, daily routines that dominate our lives while we are occupied with trivial matters, oblivious to the real issues that surround us. This song provides an apt description of the state of affairs in today's America. Americans today need to wake up to what has happened to their country and the continuing erosion of the democracy we once enjoyed. Just as in the case of average Americans being unable to see the damage done to the middle class by the Reagan administration, today, a good segment of the population seems unable to see the damage being done to our country by the Trump-led MAGA movement. The majority of the country just gave him four years to continue the destruction of our founding principles.

It should be obvious by now to all that Trump and his supporters will stop at nothing to gain and keep power. Whatever institutions stand in the way of their objective to stay in power needs to be removed right up to and including the Constitution. It should be obvious that the purpose for which they seek power is solely for self-enrichment and vindictive attacks on all who oppose them. MAGA promoters have successfully convinced many Americans that immigrants people of color, and groups who have different lifestyles or religions are a threat to the country. These groups are out to destroy America, the MAGA group will tell you, hating them is patriotism.

The country that once proudly stood with the motto inscribed on the Statue of Liberty to "Give us your tired, your poor, your huddled masses yearning to breathe free, the wretched refuse of your teeming shore" is rapidly becoming a corrupt nation filled with hate and violence. It should be no surprise that a party led by a man who worships the leadership of people like Vladimir Putin and Kim Jong Un would be out to destroy the great experiment. Perhaps at some point his supporters will realize what they have done by putting him in office again. Perhaps Autocracy is actually what the public wants.

CHAPTER 11

WHAT CAN BE DONE TO TURN THINGS AROUND

We are clearly headed in the wrong direction, and we have been since the Reagan administration. While historians can agree that President Reagan had a number of successes in his handling of foreign affairs, his domestic agenda put the country on the wrong track. There are a number of things that need to change if we are to return to the Democracy our founders envisioned. There are multiple areas that need to be addressed. The changes that will come as part of the Trump administration will only make things worse. Dramatically reducing the effectiveness of the checks and balances designed by our founders, while concentrating authority in the executive at the expense of the other two branches of government is not what our founders had in mind.

I offer here a list of suggestions not intended to be so comprehensive as to exclude other suggestions but rather a beginning point for discussion on the subject of issues that need to be addressed if we are to right the ship of state.

1 – Voting Rights

The intention of where authority would lie in the new republic was made clear by our founders it would lie in the will of the people as expressed in free and fair elections. The efforts in recent years to limit access to voting are an abomination. We must renew the effectiveness of the voting rights act. Codify in law again the sections stripped out of the original act by the Roberts Court and add a section requiring one polling place within a reasonable radius for a reasonable number of registered voters. The congestion at polling stations caused by the closing of multiple stations discourages voting.

- Outlaw gerrymandering by taking redistricting out of the hands of the state legislatures and providing specific boundary guidelines. Have a non-partisan panel of attorneys, active, and retired judges appointed by the high court in each state draw the boundary lines. As long as politicians are drawing the boundary lines, they will continue to draw the lines to protect themselves. Gerrymandering has long been an anti-democracy practice and its rampant use today is another abomination.

- Do away with the Electoral College. It is an archaic system that no longer serves a purpose. Who holds the highest office in the land should be determined by popular vote.

- Codify in federal law specific guidelines on early voting and mail-in-voting so that voting is encouraged and uniform from state to state.

2 – Money in Politics

- Overturn Citizens United and do away completely with Political Action Committees.

PACs have become impossible to properly monitor and regulate. They serve only to provide a vehicle for money to control our electoral process. PAC's are the primary vehicle by which the wealthiest individuals and corporations have taken control of our electoral process.

- Restrict fund raising to within the boundaries of the candidate's district. A Senate candidate running in a small state receiving millions in contributions from corporations and wealthy individuals in the larger more effluent states is not conducive to accountability.

- Limit contributions from any one source, including contributions from the candidates themselves.

- Limit the number of months in which a candidate can run a media campaign. Politicians would be more responsive to the needs of their constituents if they spent more time shaking hands and less time sitting with a consultant designing television commercials.

3 – Wealth Inequality

- Repeal the Trump and Bush tax cuts. The cuts were designed to benefit only the wealthy, and there is no evidence that they accomplished anything else.

- Set new progressive tax rates with those at the top paying their fair share.

- Increase the corporate tax while closing the multitude of loopholes in the current code. It is a fact that those who have the most to protect benefit the most from government services. They need to pay for the services they receive.

- Strengthen employee rights and set a livable minimum wage. A person working a forty-hour week deserves a paycheck that can provide for basic needs.

4 – Combating Misinformation

- Reassert some form of the fairness doctrine so that organizations that identify themselves as news agencies must meet standards of integrity, honesty, and fairness. Opinion and conspiracy theories should not be broadcast as legitimate news stories.

- Extend those standards to social media outlets when they are being used for political commentary and make them identify opinions as such while offering equal time to opposing opinions.

5 – Addressing Corruption

- Increase transparency by having all elected and high-ranking appointed officials make their tax returns public. No more hiding the ball, if you choose a career in public service, transparency is required. If you don't want to meet the transparency standards then stay out of government positions.

- Standards of integrity written in law for all public servants, including all members of the judiciary. Large gifts from wealthy donors, whether they are reported or not, should not be allowed.

- Term limits for Congress, as well as federal judges including the Supreme Court. Make the House of Representatives a four-year term with half the House up for election every two years. Limit House members and Senate members to three terms. Staggered five year terms for federal judges.

- Those elected to federal office, as well as those appointed to head agencies of the federal government, should be required to place their business holdings, as well as their financial investments, in a blind trust while in office in order to stop insider trading. Voting patterns by elected officials should not match their investment portfolios.

- Federal judicial appointments should not be made on the recommendation of organizations like the federalist society. Recommendations should come from a bi-partisan committee with equal representation from both political parties. The members of the committee should be appointed by the President confirmed by the Senate and made up of lawyers and retired judges. Recommendations should be made on the basis of qualifications, not political affiliations. Re – instate the requirement that judges need sixty votes for Senate confirmation. This will make it so the nominated person will need some support from the minority party in the Senate. The original intent of the sixty vote requirement was to make the appointments less political. It should have never been changed and both major parties played a part in the elimination of the sixty vote requirement.

It's tempting to call for a new constitutional convention, however, in a country as divided as this country is today, that may be a bit too dangerous. The actions that would need to be taken to implement the types of changes recommended here would require a Congress and a President with a great deal of courage. Changes of this magnitude would only come from the efforts of leaders more concerned with the future of the country than with preserving their own power. Leadership of this type is nearly nonexistent in Washington today, and that has been the case for some time. Observing our leaders on a day-to-day basis makes it very difficult to be anything but pessimistic.

The change must start with the voters turning away from the cowardly, self-serving types that currently hold the seats of power in our nation. Voters must also reject charlatans like the one we just elected, who run for the sole purpose of gaining wealth and feeding their ego. Working people electing as their salvation the man who passed the largest billionaire tax cut in history also does not inspire confidence in our future.

In his State of the Union address in 1944, FDR offered his economic bill of rights "the second bill of rights." His feeling was that this second bill of rights was necessary in order for average Americans to engage in the 'pursuit of happiness' as promised in the Constitution. His economic bill of rights included;

- Employment, there should be availability for every citizen to have gainful employment.

- An adequate income for food, shelter and recreation.

- Farmers should have the right to a fair income.

- Freedom from unfair competition and monopolies.

- Decent housing.

- Adequate medical care.

- Social security and Education.

It would be a positive step if the two major parties today had these same goals has their central focus. When Franklin Roosevelt took office, the country had truly reached rock bottom. Things had become so desperate that his agenda to turn things around was readily accepted. Perhaps we will have to reach rock bottom again as a nation for any type of collective awakening to occur. We may not be at rock bottom yet, but we are close.

ABOUT THE AUTHOR

With an education background in political science, sixteen years in elected office, and eight more years serving as a commissioner in the administration of Maine Governor John Baldacci, Jack Cashman's life has provided him with the expertise necessary to assess the state of affairs in America. Armed with this perspective, he has presented a clear and concise narrative of where we have been, where we are today, and where we are headed. He also offers a number of suggestions on how we can get back to the nation we once were, the nation our founding fathers envisioned.

Jack lives in Hampden, Maine, with his wife of more than fifty years, near his two sons and five granddaughters. The country his granddaughters will have to live in provided the basis for his concerns about the direction of our nation.

www.ingramcontent.com/pod-product-compliance
Lightning Source LLC
LaVergne TN
LVHW041658060526
838201LV00043B/486